The ABCs of Influence

Compiled by

Dr. Amanda H. Goodson

& Dr. Karockas Watkins

The ABCs of Influence
Compiled by Dr. Amanda H. Goodson and Dr. Karockas Watkins
Featured authors (in alphabetical order): Marvin Carolina (Foreword), LaKindra Frances-Jones, Dr. Amanda H. Goodson, JoAnn Johnson, Henry A. Kelly, Rosalind Longmire, Dr. Claudette Owens, Dr. Yvette Rice, Catherine Ripley, Patrice Schaffer, Sharon Wamble-King, Dr. Karockas Watkins, Janelle Wood

Editing: Adam Colwell's WriteWorks, LLC, Adam Colwell and Ginger Colwell
Book Design: Decatur Printing Solutions, LLC and Inktobook.com
Published by Amanda Goodson Global, LLC

Printed in the United States of America
ISBN (Paperback): 978-1-951501-17-4
ISBN (eBook): 978-1-951501-18-1

Acknowledgements

LaKindra Francis-Jones

I am grateful and humbled to be participate in this body of work along with the co-authors, and I would like to express my gratitude to Dr. Amanda H. Goodson for including me in this project of like-minded and brilliant leaders. To my rock, my husband, Walter, thank you for tolerating and encouraging me through all my endeavors, yet loving and supporting the journey. To my children, Logan and Tristan, I carved the paths so that I may lead by example and light the way for you to grow into your own and utilize the talents that you are blessed to behold. You all complete me! Thanks be to God for mountaintop experiences, blessings, grace, and His mercy.

Dr. Amanda H. Goodson

I'd like to thank my family for their continued support in my endeavors to write, speak, train, and coach, along with so many other things that I have the opportunity to be blessed to do. My husband, Lonnie, you are such an amazing man and you are perfect for me. To my son, Jelonni, thank you for loving me how I am and for allowing me to love you back. To my mom, sister, and extended family, thank you so very much for always being there for me. Je're, and the Goodson

Global, LLC team, thank you for your tireless support for everything I do! God gets the glory!

JoAnn Johnson

I bless the Lord, who daily loads me with benefits, even the God of my salvation. I am grateful to Him for the opportunity to be a contributor to this awe-inspiring anthology project.

Sincere gratitude to my loving and supportive husband, Deacon Leroy Johnson, who treats me like a queen each and every day. To my mother and father, Elder Bob and Carla Long, for their effectual fervent prayers. To my two phenomenal adult daughters, Heather (son-in-law Jelielk) and Leslie, whose endless respect helped me understand and acknowledge that God often chooses the unlikely to accomplish His purposes. To my gifted grandchildren, Essence, Jehiel, and Milena, for their unconditional love.

Love to my baby sister, Adrienne Armstrong, who first labeled me a "quiet storm" and helped me accept the anointing on my life, and to my other siblings and their spouses for allowing me to be the "big sister" of our family.

God's abundant blessings upon the executive and administrative leaders of R.H.E.M.A. and ADOR: Sister Marta Bester, Sister Paulene Coleman, Minister Glorene Driver, Sister Sharon Franklin, Sister Kel'ley Garner, Sister Sabrina Garner, Sister Gloria Green, Sister Latanya Grey, Minister Alice Hobbs, Sister Leslie Johnson, Minister Melanee Roper, Elder Ordel McClendon, Sister Bridget Neely, and Elder Gloria Tisdale. These Spirit-filled women masterfully caught the God-inspired ministry vision and are continuing to faithfully and joyfully run with it.

Last but certainly not least, in loving memory, my dear mother-in-law, Sally Jones, my beloved friend and godmother of my daughters, Deborah Tillman, my brother, Ronald Long, and my niece, Whitney Long, whose faith and courage in the midst of unimaginable odds have challenged and persuaded me to endure as a good soldier and press on with humility and purposeful action until my Kingdom work on this earth is done.

Henry A. Kelly

I would like to express my sincere heartfelt thanks to God who gives me daily strength and blessings, and to my wife, Joanne, and son, Philip, who have supported me immensely. To my other family members and friends, I truly thank you for your unconditional love and support. Additionally, I want to thank my First Touch Logistics family for making my dream a reality! Lastly, Dr. Goodson, what can I say but kudos for bringing this project together and inviting me to be a part of it! To those in areas of influence as a leader, thank you for all you do. Somebody's looking to you to show them the way, one step at a time.

Rosalind Longmire

Thank you all who assisted me through this incredible endeavor. Special thanks to Al, Pierce, Jarrett, my mom and sisters, and friends for your love and support through this venture. Finally, to all my mentors, coaches, and sponsors, I am truly grateful for the encouragement and opportunities that contributed to my accomplishments on my journey to purpose!

Dr. Claudette Owens

This collaboration has been a wonderful opportunity to share with and glean from a group of accomplished yet humble co-authors. Their uniqueness brought such light and fruitfulness to the table. I am grateful for such fortune to serve with them and support this amazing project. Heartfelt thanks to my dear friend, Dr. Amanda H. Goodson, who always serves as a constant source of grace and encouragement for this opportunity. Special thanks to my husband, children, grandchildren, friends, and my many mentors along the way who were kind enough to share a little part of them to help shape me.

Dr. Yvette Rice

I give God all of the glory and honor, for without Him, I could do nothing. A loving thank you to Dr. Amanda H. Goodson for pursuing the vision of this wonderful anthology. Thank you to all of the individuals who so boldly shared their stories and made this book possible. A special thank you to my husband, Bishop Sam Rice Th.D., for encouraging me to spread my wings and soar to my God-given destiny. Also, to our children Sharné, Samuel Christopher, and Amber, thank you for your loving support.

Catherine Ripley

I would like to thank all the people who have continued to influence, inspire, and motivate me. The list is long but includes my two children, Candace and Alex, and all my teachers, mentors, colleagues, bosses, authors, musicians, and leaders—spiritual, cultural, and political. I am grateful for the chance to pass on my experiences, successes, and failures so that others can learn and go on to use their own influence to make the world a better place.

Patrice Schaffer

Being part of this awesome group of authors has been one of the most rewarding experiences than I could have ever imagined. None of this would have been possible without my good friend, Marion Witte, who put me in touch with Dr. Amanda H. Goodson to be an author in this book and has helped me numerous times with great business advice. I'm so grateful for my husband, Michael, for his unconditional love, encouragement, and for always supporting my goals, even the crazy ones! Lastly, thanks to everyone at navitend who encouraged me to step out of my comfort zone and follow my marketing passion to bleed orange (navitend's theme colors).

Sharon Wamble-King

To my husband, Leon, for his unwavering love, support, fervent prayers, and effusively championing his vision of my unlimited possibilities. To my family, those of blood and love, whose prayers, loyal allegiance, acceptance and, of course, humor are continual sources of encouragement, inspiration, comfort, and joy. To my sister-friends—you know who you are—who stand by and with me, cheering me and challenging me as I navigate through every chapter of my journey. I am so grateful for your love, gracious generosity, vulnerability, insightful conversations, walking, sitting, and divinely pausing with me along my winding life path. To my mentors, coaches, and professional colleagues whose belief in my brilliance creates the safety and provides the catalyst for me to challenge my thinking, learn, grow, and evolve. To my Ph.D. colleagues who catapult me to new intellectual vistas. Most importantly, I am grateful to God, who has a plan for my life, one for good and not disaster, to give me a future and a hope. He has begun a good work in me, and He will complete it.

Dr. Karockas Watkins

I would like to acknowledge my lovely wife, Audra, who stood by my side and encouraged with this project. Also, to my family and special friends, thank you for the encouragement and support. I appreciate all the business and spiritual mentors and exceptional people who made a difference for me by seeing something special and great inside of me. I am in this place in life because of others giving of themselves into me. I am grateful to God for His grace and for you all!

Janelle Wood

I especially want to thank my Lord and Savior, Jesus Christ, for entrusting me with His work. I am grateful to my family for their continued support in all of my endeavors, whether it be to advocate, write, speak, educate, mentor, and all of the amazing opportunities

I have been blessed to pursue. Thank you to my loving and supportive husband, Andrew, my rock and best friend. I love you. To my beloved son, Bryce, thank you for words of encouragement and support. Mama loves you. To my mom, dad, sisters, brother, extended family, friends, Black Mothers Forum family and allies, I truly appreciate and love you all. Thank you, Dr. Amanda H. Goodson, for this opportunity to edify others. I am honored and deeply humbled to be a part of this inspiring and powerful work with these amazing and courageous co-authors.

A Note from the Authors

We are saddened about the current situation in the United States. The impact of the COVID-19 pandemic and social unrest have deeply wounded our nation and its people. We believe it will be through active and genuine people of influence that we can get to a renewed place of peace and wholeness as a country and as Americans.

October 2020

Table of Contents

Foreword

Direction of Change

I WAS JUST out of college with my industrial management degree from the Georgia Institute of Technology when I had my first professional encounter with a person of influence.

I didn't know anyone when I went to work for Oscar Mayer in Portland, Oregon. But one of the people I worked with, Dan, took me under his wing and showed me what I needed to do to be successful. He helped me to understand the corporate structure and the processes and procedures of the company from a sales perspective. He often asked me to meet him for breakfast or lunch, and sometimes invited me to dinner with his family since I didn't have any family in Portland.

I recall one time when I messed up the pudding snack displays in three different grocery stores, and the senior vice president of one of the stores yelled at him about it. Dan came down hard on me, I fixed the problem, and we moved forward. But I often use that story today as an example of how I could have crumbled. I could have been upset at him and disappointed in myself, but I wasn't. I knew, while some may have been seen his actions as harsh, Dan was trying to help me—to influence me in the direction he knew would be best for me.

That's one of the things influencers do, isn't it? Influence is the ability to move people in the direction you think is best for them. Whether it was during my early career in sales and leadership at Oscar Mayer and Kraft Foods, Carolina Beverage Distributing, and Sears; in my 25 years of service as vice president of diversity at J.E. Dunn Construction; or today as president and CEO of the Better Business Bureau of Greater Kansas City and in my work as a public speaker, trainer, and consultant, I have both benefitted from influence and been an influencer in the lives of others.

From bosses to teammates and younger professionals, I have influenced people throughout my life and career. To increase my own influence, I've tried to find those who are doing great things and strive to keep pace with or overtake them so I can better myself and broaden my reach as an influencer. I am able to look down the road to see what no others clearly can. It's something I have used over the years to help me influence organizations as well as individuals in moving forward.

Like many others, I have had a roller coaster of a life. I have messed some things up. I have done some really good things. I've been up and down, but I can still stand. That gives me confidence and credibility with people. In the end, I've found a way to succeed—and so can you. The stories Dr. Amanda H. Goodson and Dr. Karockas Watkins have compiled in this book will show you how to be influenced and to become an influencer. It'll help you enjoy the rewards of influence, where you see someone you helped grow and bloom. Knowing you had something, whether a little bit or a lot, to do with that is priceless.

Take the insights and lessons learned from *The ABCs of Influence,* apply them routinely, and you will become an agent of change in a world that desperately needs you.

Marvin Carolina, Jr.

President and CEO, Better Business Bureau of Greater Kansas City

Move the Needle!

WHEN IT COMES to business jargon, "moving the needle" has been around for quite a while. It's an idiom that calls to mind the volume gauge on an old radio or the needle on the speedometer of an older model car. However you picture it, though, its meaning is clear and as fresh as ever.

By pure definition, to move the needle is to "change a situation to a noticeable degree"—and that is exactly what you do as an influencer.

It is our passion to inspire and equip you to become an influencer of individuals, or organizations, to such a degree of excellence that your competition is rendered *irrelevant*. When you shift the direction and create the thrust to take a person, or a business, from being mediocre or average to succeeding and in high demand, you'll not only set yourself apart from the pack, but you'll accelerate ahead of it. Even more, you'll make a genuine and lasting difference as you change the culture and reform the landscape as others notice and *need* what only you can provide.

The ABCs of Influence will introduce you to 12 fabulous and gifted individuals who are influencers in their domains, displaying the power to lead, bargain, change people's minds, and show who they are and what they can do.

LaKindra Francis-Jones speaks from her role as director of mission assurance and quality at a major aerospace engineering company to show you how influence is all about relationships—and it should extend beyond our typical business lingo in terms of partnerships.

Dr. Amanda H. Goodson details how everyone can be an influencer as they learn and understand the three types or ways to influence—negative, positive, and transformational—to become people focused servant leaders who think outside of the box yet don't necessarily leave the ground.

JoAnn Johnson describes how your impact as an influencer will be based on the appeal you have to affect other people's thinking, actions, and development, as well as the trust and confidence they have in your competence and your understanding of their needs and their interests.

Henry A. Kelly shares how influence has shaped his life and career, and reveals how positive influence drives his current business as a delivery partner for a large logistics company so that you can learn how to deliver your best to someone else so that everyone benefits.

Rosalind Longmire talks about how she has influenced others to excel and rise higher, especially in their spiritual lives, so they can move forward. You'll discover how your ability to impact the conduct, nature, or character of a person can help them grow and reach a desired outcome.

Dr. Claudette Owens tells how her personal mission statement informs how she influences others as a consultant, and that it is your passion for people and desire to see each one bring out the greatness inside of them that will propel you forward to impact others.

Dr. Yvette Rice speaks about influence as having an effect on the character, development, or behavior of someone to the point of adding value to their lives from a developmental perspective and demonstrating the importance of integrity upon who they are and what they do.

Catherine Ripley explores discerning when you are using power versus influence and how knowing the difference and applying it to how you interact with others will determine the amount of influence you have, how it is received, and how it will define the tone of your organization.

Patrice Schaffer shares how she has been blessed beyond her imaginings as an influencer both personally and professionally, and she exhorts you to know that your best is more than enough as long as you continue to prioritize relationships with others.

Sharon Wamble-King talks about the different outcomes of influence and how the ability to motivate, inspire, compel, shift beliefs and attitudes, and reframe paradigms will produce results that change the way people see the world and interact with others.

Dr. Karockas Watkins tells how being an influencer starts with looking for opportunities, thinking about them, and discerning what opportunities are best so that you can then be willing to speak up, step in, and step out to place yourself in that situation.

Finally, Janelle Wood speaks about influence as being able to model the characteristics you want others to exhibit. She describes great influencers as being focused and kind, humble servants who are confident but not conceited and are willing to do what they ask others to do.

Being an influencer happens when you learn to get in the room, get to the table, and make an impact. Influencers know they have to be around people who have learned the "code," the other way of thinking that takes them to a different sphere of living. Influence is not a popularity contest. You don't need to have a well-known name or a massive social media presence. True influence is about having the power to move people to another level as they look at you in a way that shows they honor and respect what you say and what you bring to the table. True influence positions you to have an effect on other decision makers because your proven record of being an agent of change and a purveyor of prosperity is apparent.

As you read *The ABCs of Influence,* you will discover that influencers are people of integrity who can lead from any chair. Influencers leverage those around them and surround themselves with people as good as, or better than, they are. Influencers are also servants who are willing to learn, listen to people who have gone before them, and stretch themselves. Once others recognize you as an influencer, they will tell their colleagues (and other influencers) to listen to what you have to say, increasing your impact.

As an influencer, you are not like everybody else. You are a solution provider. You are a strategist. You are an executor. You have a competitive advantage. However, we are in a world of change and complexity, so you need to put yourself out there and take some risks. As an influencer, you also have to be willing to walk alone and take the hits. When you are not staying within the box others have placed around you, you become an odd bird, even a threat. For everyone who says you are great, there may be double the amount of people questioning you. You've got to be fine with that because you know who you are and who you are called to be.

You'll know you are an influencer when people, or organizations, come to you to help them get from A to Z. They know you have the structured ability and knowledge to do it, and if you don't, you have someone in your network who can. Then, once you embrace your capacity as an influencer, you maintain your position by being humble and firm, keeping pace, and staying on course. In addition, you need to continually examine your passion and your "why," knowing both give you the energy you need to be an expert at knowing the global landscape and navigating the terrain.

It is then that your competition becomes irrelevant—and you move the needle!

We hope you enjoy *The ABCs of Influence* and are encouraged and persuaded by the stories you are about to read.

Dr. Amanda H. Goodson
Dr. Karockas Watkins

The next anthology book from Amanda Goodson Global on Resilience is scheduled for release in 2022.

1

Elevate to Motivate

LaKindra Frances-Jones

THE ABILITY TO elevate your views or vision in a manner that motivates and encourages others is influence. Influence demands that leaders collaborate with people to strategize and share views, value systems, priorities, and principles, then steer others to help them succeed. Because it requires putting in the effort to corral everyone around a task or mission, influence is all about relationships—and it should extend beyond our typical business lingo in terms of partnerships. Influence is a major attribute of great leadership that goes beyond persuasion and draws people in. Influential leaders foster environments where creativity and innovation flows and people and organizations flourish. In the end, influence happens through how you cultivate relationships with others through your engagement, involvement, and presence, not merely your title or authority.

In my role as director of mission assurance and quality at a major aerospace engineering company, I influence others and face challenges by engaging and collaborating the organization and working with leaders, peers, and direct reports. Influential leaders serve others and shape opportunities for their organizations and teams to win. Shaping requires leaders to discuss and explain the "why." It is essential to define the bigger picture, provide direction, and demonstrate alignment to the task at hand in order to bring everyone together and to determine the right path forward for impact and success. Influential leadership requires faith and courage as people are hesitant and resistant to change because they wonder, "How is this going to impact me?" "Who is going to pay for this?" "What am I going to get from this?" Being able to respond in a timely manner, identify issues early, course correct, and implement the corrective actions provides others the opportunity to grow and fosters trust. Leading through influence gives your organization a voice which allows them to readily communicate challenges as well as the improvements required. This takes a tremendous amount of collaboration and cooperation, and it also provides opportunities to build social capital. As I've influenced my leaders, peers, and teams, they've embraced ideas and solutions as part of their primary initiatives, and we are all able to continue to communicate progress and concerns, as well as what we need to do, to be successful.

I've learned three vital lessons as an influencer. First, I've had to separate people from the problem. If I am going to lead effectively, I must assess and speak to the areas we need to improve rather than to the person or group of individuals I believe may be barriers to the situation or the issue. If I associate the issue with the person or group, there could be others who may feel isolated and can take personal offense. However, if I speak to the impact on the project, program, organization, or business, then I create an open dialogue for people to step up and say, "Well, you know what? I have a team or a program in mind within my organization that may be able to solve the problem."

As the mission assurance leader for an experimental development program, my team and I were required to develop a unique system checkout and sell-off process to accommodate quick reaction capability development hardware for delivery to the customer to conduct experimental testing and demonstrations. Unfortunately, there was no precedence of this being performed in our organization. So, I focused on identifying personnel with experience in testing, verification, validation, and system sell-off for delivery rather than bringing attention to the lack of existing procedural documentation. Additionally, I did not put any energy into challenging team members about leveraging process documentation from other innovation projects. I leaned in, presented the risks relative to resource needs to generate the documentation, and reminded everyone of the relevance of this data to support product delivery to our customer. In a matter of days, we secured key personnel who were eager to engage and generate process procedural tasks that directly contributed to product selloff to the customer and leveraged existing procedures from research and development programs that had a history of successful demos and deliveries to the customer.

Second, as a leader, I definitely have to *commit to being in the driver's seat.* For example, my husband, Walter, and I both work for the same company. While we serve in different departments with different job roles and responsibilities, we both find that we have similar leadership challenges. We are each working with and leading people, and we're trying to influence rather than just guide them to action. That is the space we operate in, so we have to learn to effectively influence people by being sensitive to peoples' pride, respectful of others' ideas and opinions, providing honest and sincere feedback while being active listeners, and praising improvement.

When Walter and I relocated and transferred to Huntsville, Alabama for work, he transitioned into a new product line and program team. In addition to developing relationships in a new customer community, he recognized that he needed to form and build up a solid logistics team capable of frontline customer engagement and support that will exceed their expectations and grow the business. He started by working with the current team and setting clear goals for the organization and then following suit by assigning employees specific goals to direct their focus. When Veronica joined the team, she was eager to succeed and utilize her engineering technical talent. Walter recognized that she was a very capable and talented woman but also understood the importance of establishing specific goals for Veronica that were attainable and results-oriented to drive higher performance. Throughout their working relationship, there were challenges related to customer requests for technical analyses and reporting. Oftentimes, Veronica seemed frustrated with the antics and tone of the criticism of her work from her peers and other team members. Walter saw that these interactions left her feeling deflated and demotivated, so he made an effort to partake in the details of her work, utilized misunderstandings to accentuate positive improvement, and offered sincere praise and appreciation for her contributions. Simply put, he routinely engaged

Veronica and the team, gave them credit for their work, provided feedback and recommendations for improvement, praised their efforts, and rewarded their successes.

Motivation and morale coincide with influence as well. The age old adage still applies: treat people the way you want to be treated. In essence, in order to lead well, we must serve well. As a servant leader, I often ask myself, "What can I give?" I believe that my level of involvement is directly tied to my level of engagement. There will always be troubling times when we are juggling tasks and shifting priorities in order to meet deadlines. Influential leaders are comfortable with being uncomfortable, and they can separate people from the problem and define the issue as a shared problem.

My life has been positively impacted by other influencers. From a personal perspective, it all ties back to my family, especially my grandmother, Velma Francis. I come from a matriarchal family in Louisiana, where women predominantly hold the leadership roles in the home and provide examples of strength and courage. My grandmother only had a fourth-grade education, yet she was able to attain gainful employment, buy her own home, and raise her children and several grandchildren. Ms. Velma, as she was commonly called, was a tenacious woman of faith with unwavering courage in her convictions. I still remember her kneeling on the side of her bed prior to sunrise and late at night, praying for grace and mercy and speaking blessings and favor over our lives. My grandmother instilled a strong sense of purpose in me that I took to heart. Her work ethics and morals were reflected in everything she embodied and endured, and no matter the circumstance, she always treated people with respect. What I witnessed is that Ms. Velma overcame most obstacles through passion, persistence, and discipline. She was a baby boomer from a sharecropping family, and she was required to do laborious and often punishing manual labor, which prevented her from regularly attending school. Therefore, she didn't readily look to education as a primary differentiator for opportunities and survival. On the other hand, my mother, Brenda, was hopeful, a teenage mother who didn't go on to complete her secondary education because her responsibilities to be a provider and homemaker were her priority. Unfortunately, her job prospects were very limited, which curtailed her income earning potential and extended into every facet of our lives, from housing and schools to resources.

As a result, my generation had a paradigm shift, knowing we were going to have to work smarter rather than physically harder, and be educated in order to compete at the next level. For me, this was accomplished through the relationships I developed with teachers and counselors who recognized my potential. These teachers were more than just educators. They were influential leaders. They were my offensive line through my teenage and young adult life, the kind of leaders that I have found to be the most credible source of influencers. They were effective communicators with a keen sense of awareness of their class and school environments, and they had the ability to meet students on their level without comprising their principles. They were patient yet persistent, disciplined, and organized, which were skills and qualities that I emulated and adopted to prepare for my future.

Professionally, I was a mid-career program manager by the time I met Duane Gooden. He was the first African American executive in his specific area at the company, and he made a point to connect with me and recognize the value of sponsorship and his responsibility to groom and advocate for rising, high performing professionals. Duane recognized that my career experiences provided a unique perspective to organizational challenges and wanted to promote and accelerate my professional development and growth. If it wasn't for Duane's intentional and purposeful actions and efforts on my behalf, I wouldn't be at the director level today. Now that I've accomplished more than half of my career milestones, it has become much more important for me to pull up other people, particularly women and people of color. I want to give them opportunities to be in the room, to understand leadership dialogue, and see the strategic significance of where the business is heading and how leaders interact and exchange ideas around the room as decisions are made.

I believe the one's leadership style causes people to influence differently in various situations. I have seen a majority of leaders successfully influence through an authoritative leadership style because it was directive. When you're direct, people know and understand exactly what your expectations are. One previous leader managed down through the organization, meaning she encouraged and required regular face-to-face or phone communication with the directors within our organization. A more recent leader managed up, looking to his peer community and above through the corporate chain to understand what was going on. They were two people with completely different leadership styles, but each worked for them, and their organizations were both effective and successful.

My leadership style is more democratic. I am very interested in understanding how my goals, directions, initiatives, and plans impact the organization, and I encourage my organization to actively participate in identifying our strategic priorities yearly. In addition, although I believe some individuals possess the ability to successfully navigate through a myriad of circumstances, their ability to connect and influence is still attributed to their experiences and exposure. So, influential leaders are taught, not born, as influence is a learned behavior. This is evidenced in every professional field as well as in our daily lives. The ultimate reward of being an influencer is creating a legacy. My legacy is my impact and the impression that I made on the lives of individuals that I've encountered in both personal and professional circles. Legacy reminds me of the sacrifices and successes an individual has achieved that can bestow hope, grace, and inspiration to and from one generation to the next. Another reward of being an influencer is that the brilliance and light of others whom you have impacted and motivated will continue to stimulate and burn within you as well as in them.

My future as an influencer to cultivate the vision, values, mission, and goals of my organizations to spark creativeness and improve business performance. Additionally, I intend to expand my influence to encourage the next generation of women and minority STEM (science, technology, engineering, and math) leaders.

Sometimes, God elevates us to a place where we are in a room with distinguished and esteemed leaders. His only task is for us to be still, listen, and learn. If you are going to be a person of influence, you will need to seek the Lord for guidance and the ability to decipher recognize when it is time to be still, listen, and learn—and when it is time to influence and lead with a voice that stirs hearts, souls, and minds, and prompts others to action.

LaKindra Frances-Jones is director of mission assurance and quality at a major aerospace engineering company who has served in both program leadership and engineering positions during her 20-plus year career. She has received a variety of awards for her excellence in the aerospace and defense industry community, and she's recognized for outstanding professional and community partnerships and relationships. LaKindra holds both bachelor's and master's degrees in physics from Southern University A&M College, and a master's degree in business administration from Webster University. Contact LaKindra at lakindrafjones@gmail.com

2

Dream Big, Think Big, and Transact Big

Dr. Amanda H. Goodson

EVERYBODY CAN BE an influencer. I have heard leadership expert John C. Maxwell state that everything rises and falls on leadership—and that leadership is influence: nothing more, nothing less. I believe some of your influence comes as a result of what you've learned along the way. Other aspects of your ability to influence are innate. It is just part of your fiber. It is mapped into your DNA. I have learned there are three types or ways to influence—negative, positive, and transformational—and as you dream big, think big, and transact big, you will experience each one.

As a senior leader for a major defense contractor and in my previous professional positions (including my tenure as the first African American woman to ever hold the position of Director of Safety and Mission Assurance at the National Aeronautics and Space Administration, or NASA), I've been in meetings where someone obviously had a bad day or something was just not right within my team. It created *negative influence* against the direction we were going. Sometimes, I have had to make unpopular decisions which impacted the team negatively (in the short run). Finally, there have been times when I've been out in the community and overheard a store clerk or other worker saying negative things about their boss, a fellow employee, or even about other customers. That had a negative influence on me and on my experience at that store. In general, negative influence is not desirable.

On the other hand, I've had and seen certain leaders whose style was so amazing that I had a positive experience that fueled a desire for me to do things better and want to be the best. *Positive influence* is evidenced when someone has led you to your goal and your passion or towards the direction where you can do wonderful things. Pierce Longmire is a student working toward a major and a doctorate in molecular medicine. I was able to have a positive influence with him as we went through my *Unlock Your Full Potential* coaching program and the "FRESH WILL" characteristics of the Goodson 9 Block to develop a life strategy that would make his goals and dreams an achievable reality. I asked Pierce to "become" his future self, 10 years in the future, looking at every one of his goals from the perspective of what he wanted to have already accomplished by *then.* Next, I asked him to work backwards from year ten, to year nine, then eight, then seven, and so on, all the way to where he was in the present. It was a revolutionary process for him. He knew what he wanted to do, but he had never seen himself as a person that would add to the body of knowledge in a way that I knew he could.

Currently, Pierce is a researcher. He had begun working as a student studying viruses. Pierce had never imagined himself contributing to a solution for a regional medical problem that could have global implications, but he did. Through my coaching, I influenced Pierce, who is an introvert, to work on his public speaking and presence. We had mock sessions where he'd get up and speak about something associated with science biology. He also needed practice to write papers so he could be published in periodicals, and we worked on that together. My positive influence on Pierce was to get him outside of his comfort zones to start becoming the person that he is going to be!

Then there's *transformational influence*. This causes us to change our total mindset. A simple example of this came when me and a colleague were coaching a young person. He had a ring in his nose and a hairstyle that we knew, for better or worse, would be unacceptable in certain professional environments that this individual wanted to impact. We taught him about workplace behaviors and the realities of transitioning from college to corporate life. At the next session, the young person returned with no nose ring, a haircut, and a shave. The physical transformation was apparent, and it better positioned him to be effective in the workplace. When I was at NASA, I intentionally changed how I dressed, and even my hairstyle, to give myself a more executive presence that I knew was necessary in order for me to succeed and have the most influence.

A better example of transformational influence, though, is when an individual learns and cultivates a skill they didn't possess before so that they can develop and get the job they desire. Je're Harmon was a really good student in high school and went off to college to major in engineering. Although she is very talented and brilliant, she found the classes to be different and harder than what she experienced in high school. Being at such a big university with plenty of distractions was more difficult than she expected it to be. Before long, she left school and returned home, but she wasn't dejected. She was proactive and worked several odd jobs before ending up at a company specializing in inventory for retailers. She travelled to stores throughout her city and surrounding communities, establishing such an excellent reputation that she became a supervisor overseeing a team of people. Je're found the job to be satisfying, and she thought she was successful because she was a supervisor.

Then I had a conversation with her. We agreed that she would never get the benefits of a full-time employee such as a 401(k). Finally, she didn't have a plan of action for later on in life. I told her, "You need to get a real job."

She looked at me, surprised. "I have a job," she replied, but she also saw something else: potential. As she started applying for other jobs, I encouraged Je're to visualize in her mind what she wanted to do and what kind of job she wanted to have. I directed her to write a letter to herself stating the goals for the type of job she desired. She discovered she had to dress differently, speak differently, and have a different attitude. She ended up getting a job at a major U.S. defense contractor in security—and she loved it! Now she has a 401(k) and is saving for her retirement. In addition, Je're returned to school to finish her degree. Je're is a leader. She has people working for her. She is a respected professional trusted to travel all over the United States on the company's behalf. It's so exciting!

Just as there are three types of influence, I have identified three dimensions of influence: internal, external, and positional/transactional. As the title suggests, *internal influence* is inside of you. It's where you influence yourself through self-talk, training, and coaching or mentoring to gain the knowledge, skills, and direction that creates the *depth* you need to impact your decisions, behaviors, and your self-image and self-esteem. It is how you build your ability to stick with things and go from one place to another. When we had to shelter in place during the coronavirus pandemic, I decided I was going to leverage it as much as possible to build my depth and better myself. I took coaching, classes, and even started a new exercise program. *External influence*, of course, is outside of yourself and represents how you can extend your influence upon individuals, your workplace, or your community as far as your passion can take you. It gives you *width* as an influencer. I had a good friend, who is a vice president of human resources, take a took at my resume and cover letter as I sought to update them after nearly 15 years. She influenced me to think differently about how I communicated who I was. She taught me how to use action verbs in ways that would be meaningful to the reader and how to prioritize my employment experience in a way that would be more relatable to an organization. It helped me extend my width as an influencer.

Positional/transactional influence speaks to being a director, a leader, or a person who is head over something in the community (including a household) that then gives you transactional influence over a group of people. That group ranges from customers and clients to other community workers and family members. Positional/transactional influence gives you *height* as an influencer. For example, my book editor works with my content, and together we have a transactional experience to create copy that elevates our shared influence on our readers. I also think of Susan, a manager of diversity and inclusion at a major contractor. Her job is to make presentations to new employees and travel to conferences to create an environment where people feel they are valued, included, and part of the team through their experiences, learning, and skills. Susan influenced interested folks in other organizations to make presentations and to go on trips with her to represent diversity and inclusion. In the process, she created a team of people to help her get the job done well. Her positional/transactional influence brought other people in so that they could influence the workplace and the community in a positive, essential way.

Influence can last for different durations of time. It can be short-term or initial, such as a consultation call where I influence a colleagues one time and have a minor but marked impact. It could be mid-term or seasonal, where my interaction with someone lasts only a matter of weeks or months but my influence and its impact are measurable and more significant. Finally, it could be long-term or lifetime, where someone such as a parent, pastor, coach, or mentor has an influence over a course of years or decades and has a major impact. I remember some of the things my mom, Mable, said when I was 10 years old, and I still apply them. She's had a long-term influence in my life. She taught me life is not always fair and that I have to work hard, sometimes twice as hard, to push toward a goal. She taught me not to look behind or beside me, but to look ahead and keep my eyes on the mark. My mom also taught me not to measure myself by the success of others. "Once you have done your best," she told me, "then you can't give any more, so don't beat yourself up if you have done your best. If you have not done your best, then you have more to give." Thanks to her, I measure myself by what I am capable of doing and by what I can do better.

There are a variety of *systems* that influence us. We operate in an economic system that influences how and when we buy and sell. We have a political system that influences the society in which we live. There are cultural influences within a society or an organization that impacts how we behave, and there is an educational system that provides the additional training we need to accomplish our goals and desires. From environmental to legal to judicial, these systems are in place, and we are part of each system in some way or another—which means we can also have influence in any of these systems.

When trainer, consultant, and author Marvin Carolina, Jr. (writer of the Foreword for this book) ended up president and CEO of the Better Business Bureau (BBB) in Kansas City, Missouri, he wanted to change the way the BBB did business so it could be a forerunner in mentoring businesses to improve. I influenced this system by helping him develop a model for that mentoring program so that the businesses that are really good were positioned to mentor the ones that needed help by targeting a problem and providing solutions. Marvin was the visionary for the comprehensive mentorship program, and I extensively worked with him to help him design and deploy it. In the end, it created a better ecosystem for businesses in the community to allow them to be successful in ways that they couldn't otherwise do on their own. Meanwhile, a specific system that influenced me has been the National Speakers Association. It taught me how to use new methods to develop content for training and development. I discovered that people like to learn in vignettes. They like pictures. They like videos. I learned how to teach something, provide a story, and deliver a call to action in three minutes or less. That system enabled me to think differently.

I'm convinced the best influencers focus on hopes and dreams. They also look to influence the most people for the longest amount of time and for the greater good. That allows everyone to be inspired and exposed, leveraged to do their best, get the best, and be the best—to be truly transformational. The best influencers also use discernment to look forward, then go back and use hindsight to influence where they are right now, and gain revelation to know something that was previously hidden. Motivational speaker and author, Les Brown, taught me that if I'm going after something that I'm absolutely passionate about, I've got to be hungry. He says if you are not hungry, then you are like everybody else, and you won't get it.

That said, it's also true that we're sometimes going to fall short, and leadership expert, speaker, coach, and author John Maxwell counsels in his book, *Fail Forward,* that we need to fail forward, meaning that we need to keep moving forward and not look behind, even though we may stumble along the way. Brown says that when we fall we should fall on our back, because when we do, we are looking up—and when we look up, we can get up. I love those kinds of insights and revelations.

Finally, I believe influencers are people focused servant leaders who think outside of the box yet don't necessarily leave the ground. They are able to take a wide, big picture look at things and be a visionary of what is coming. They understand that to influence others, they have to differentiate themselves from others, and they are engaged in long-term, intentional thinking, not short-term, reactionary responses.

I always love to share the story from my book *Astronomical Leadership* about a person who had one of the biggest influences in my professional life, Wiley Bunn. He was a slightly balding fellow who always smoked a pipe, usually protruding out of the side of his mouth. Sometimes brash in his tone, he was smart, and unlike most other high-ranking supervisors I'd met then as a young engineer at NASA, Wiley was genuinely concerned about learning more about his employees than just their immediate job duties. He often pressed us about our goals and ambitions, and while his brusqueness offended some, it didn't bother me at all. In fact, I rather liked him.

He called me in one afternoon to give him the latest update on an experiment I had been chosen to observe and report back to him about. It wasn't the first time I'd been in his office, but I was still taken aback by the sheer size of it. I guess the space was fitting for one holding his position: Director of Quality Assurance, to be expanded later to Safety and Mission Assurance.

I sat down across from him at the massive conference table. He took a puff from his pipe.

"What do you want to do?" he asked.

"What do you mean?"

"I mean, what do you really want—here at NASA?"

I thought about it and heard a voice within exhort me. *Be bold.*

I leaned forward in my chair. "I want your job."

He blew out a billow of smoke and laughed as if he were thinking I had no idea what I was asking.

"You want my job?"

"Yes, sir!"

He swiveled in his chair and looked straight ahead, as though assessing me as much as his response. His gaze wasn't skeptical, though. It was credulous. Respectful.

"I've been looking for someone to help, to create a legacy." He paused. "Okay. If you want my job, you're gonna have to work hard, do the jobs you never want to do, and do the jobs others are not willing to do."

Suddenly, I was the one challenged to take him seriously. Was he really going to give me the chance to go after his position? "I can do all those things."

He got up from his chair, and I rose from mine. "All right, then. I've got some work to do to make this happen. And no complaining from you, okay?"

"Yes, sir."

As I left Wiley's office, my mind was buzzing. *I need to do what others can't. Do what others won't. Find a space where nobody is and cannot touch where I am.*

I had been newly inspired to become an influencer at NASA. I did just that—and eventually I had Wiley's job, and I was the first African American woman to hold that position. Wiley, and other influencers like him, such as Myles Munroe and Art Stephenson, have caused me to change the way I think, catapulting me forward so that I say to myself, *I don't want to go back!* My hope and my faith were influenced in a way that I could dream big, think big, and transact big.

Being an influencer is rewarding. I see other people grow and bring change in an organization, and I watch people teach differently. In the future, I want to continue to learn, run, leap, and soar as an influencer. I desire to stay relevant, to stay healthy, and to create a compelling future for others as a mentor and coach. I hope to understand the gifts and graces on my life, and how I can incorporate those into a learning platform for other people to follow.

In the end, I believe we have a genetic code inside us to influence us. From birth, we have it in us. It causes us to be unique in our passions, our abilities, and our skills—and that results in our level of influence being at a higher level than we realize. As we continue to hope and dream, we will become the magnificent person and influencer we are supposed to be.

Dr. Amanda H. Goodson is a groundbreaking aerospace engineer who soared to become the first woman to hold the position of Director of Safety and Mission Assurance out of the Marshall Space Flight Center at NASA. Transformed from a young African American girl who was told by her teacher that she would not amount to much, Dr. Goodson uses her unstoppable "can do" spirit to inspire others to achieve their goals regardless of the obstacles.

Noted nationally for her achievements, Dr. Goodson is the recipient of the Southwest Alliance for Excellence Leadership Award; the Tucson's Woman on the Move Award for Leadership, Achievements, and Continuous Improvement in the Workplace; the Exceptional Service Medal; the Federal Employee Supervisor of the Year Award; and the Director's Commendation for Leadership Excellence in Safety, Quality, and Mission Assurance at NASA.

Dr. Goodson has served as the board of director's chair for Advancing Minorities Interest in Engineering (AMIE), a national consortium for industry, government, and academia. In addition to serving in a leadership position for a Fortune 500 aerospace company, Dr. Goodson is the senior pastor at Trinity Temple CME Church in Tucson, Arizona. Contact Amanda at amandagoodsonglobal@gmail.com

3

A Quiet Storm of Influence

JoAnn Johnson

OVER THE YEARS, people have described me as being a "quiet storm," so much so that I have adopted it as my personal catch phrase—and why not? A storm suggests action and even turbulence, and I've certainly dealt with my share of both.

I spent over 30 years in project/process management and consulting for communications corporations. I worked on the operations side of the sales team in an organization that was considered the principal consultants for other major communications companies. I built partnerships with those companies, met their needs, and helped them make their profits. Then, after I retired in 1999 at age 50, I turned my attention to being and building disciples for Jesus Christ. In 2013, I founded R.H.E.M.A. (Retired Heroines Ever Magnifying the Almighty, Inc.), where I help other women be disciple makers. Once they become a disciple of Jesus, their passion for others to know Christ becomes a priority. Studying the Word of God, they come to understand the importance of training someone else and subsequently influencing them through their actions and their lifestyles, to perpetuate that. It's a snowballing effect, done for the glory of God, so that He might be known.

My pre- and post-retirement activities, seasoned with the addition of my husband, Leroy, my two daughters, Heather and Leslie, and our three grandchildren, Essence, Jehiel, and Milena, have brought flavor and substance to my quietly stormy life—one that I'm humbled to acknowledge has also been a life of amazing influence.

Influence speaks to my ability to impact other people's thinking, actions, and development because they see me as being credible to them. Your impact as an influencer will be based on the appeal you have to that person or the trust and confidence they have in your competence and your understanding of their needs and their interests. During my undergraduate years at the University of Illinois, I met a phenomenal young woman named Joyce. As we navigated the on-campus life of dorm living, sorority events, and study groups, we became friends. Following my graduation in 1970, our different career paths kept us physically apart for over 40 years, allowing us to only occasionally see or talk to one another.

Joyce and I reconnected in 2015 when she was led to attend a R.H.E.M.A. ministry conference I hosted in Chicago, Illinois. Believing in the work of the ministry, and understanding from years of executive government experience and being on numerous corporate boards that more could be done with additional resources, Joyce encouraged us to become a non-profit, tax exempt entity, and we trusted in each other's confidence and competence to make the transition successfully. Since the year following our change to 501(c)3 status, God has blessed R.H.E.M.A. with many generous partners, enabling the ministry to provide numerous scholarships and support the work of other community organizations.

From a spiritual perspective, I have influenced others through my commitment to find out what pleases God and then do it, and I know that God is pleased when other people come to know Him and grow in Him. Therefore, I focus on mentoring women of all ages and helping them mature in Christ through their situations, circumstances, fears, and challenges—the quiet storms they face—in life. Many of them have very difficult lives, and I try to help them see their worth and their value, move beyond their challenges, and gain strength and understanding to learn from those challenges. I want them to recognize that those storms don't have to limit them in their lives and in the raising of their families.

One woman, Gloria, sent me a note in March 2020, saying, "You have encouraged me when I thought I couldn't do anything and had given up on myself. You have challenged me to allow God to lead me, and I have assurance from you that if anyone can do God's work, I can do it, too. I know that God will give me what I need, and He will not allow me to fail when I am working for Him. I know that I still have a long way to go because I am still growing, but I have the desire to do good."

After God and His Word, the most significant influencers in my life begin with my parents, Bob and Carla Long. Both are committed servants in their faith. Dad was a preacher who could be found studying for sermons, teaching Sunday school, and visiting the sick in hospitals or homebound church members. Mom was usually volunteering at the local school Parent Teacher Association, training church youth ushers, or canvasing the neighborhood with the Mother's Club inviting children to come to Sunday school.

My parents were born and raised in the south, which gave them a keen sense of family and community. Neither of them were college educated, but they had a strong work standard. My parents nurtured my spiritual growth and self-awareness through Christian education, music and dance lessons, Girl Scouts, and higher education. Being married for over 70 years, they are a phenomenal example of a healthy marriage. Thanks to mom and dad, I know that I have purpose and that my walk must line up with my talk if I am going to have a positive impact on humanity. My life must glorify God.

Professionally, my greatest influencer was my former boss, Robert Nibbs. He was an executive at a major communications company when I was an entry level manager. He was the type of person who respected people and property. He took the time to make people feel valued and could often be seen casually interacting with all levels of staff, including the janitorial workers, and overheard asking them about their families. While waiting for the elevator, you might find him picking up a small piece of paper off the floor and placing it in the trash. It was under his leadership that I was promoted to operations director—and when he heard I was leaving the company, Robert tapped me to do consulting with the company he was working for at that time. Robert believed in reaching back and helping people to achieve. Because of his example, I came to understand that effective mentoring, counseling, and coaching has to be done in a spirit of unconditional love to see someone develop to their full potential.

I believe that one of the most important responsibilities

of an influencer is to not betray the trust of others. You should always observe confidentiality. You should have integrity, be truthful, and have strong ethics. Another responsibility is to create a comfortable environment for a two-way dialogue with the people you are trying to influence where you can affirm and celebrate them. Since 2001, my husband and I have been certified marriage enrichment workshop leaders through Marriage Enrichment, Inc. As the group facilitator, I am required to create an atmosphere of trust using specifically worded instructions so that the overall process will be a positive and successful enrichment experience for the couples.

I've learned over the years that one must be trusted in order to be truly heard. Michelle and her husband, Doug, had a good marriage, but after 10 years, Michelle felt like their marriage could be even better. Although Doug agreed to attend an enrichment workshop, I could see his tension and reluctance to participate during their initial interactive exercises. I was able to gain Doug's trust as I allowed him to move through the weekend at his own pace, reinforcing the instructions as we went and letting him confirm what was requested of him as needed. As we moved through the exercises, I had many opportunities to affirm Doug's participation. At the conclusion of the workshop, I congratulated Doug for his efforts. His body language indicated that he was pleased with himself as he promised to faithfully utilize the tools he had learned.

Finally, if something is confusing, ask clarifying questions. Try to be uplifting and not opinionated, making sure you understand the needs of others as you try to help them be better or influence what they are doing. When Leroy and

I retired to Tucson, Arizona, I knew God had more work for me to do. I believed in the power of prayer, but I never imagined that I would wind up serving as a prayer coordinator at Family Life Radio, an international Christian radio network. The prayer coordinator's constituents could be co-workers or listeners who called, emailed, or stopped by the office to share their prayer needs. Our task was to pray with them about their troubles and concerns. Many had unimaginable hurts and challenges. As I listened to each request, I had to silently ask God to reveal to me the words or scripture to soothe their pain and reach their aching hearts. Many contacted me so often that we became like family.

In 2018, R.H.E.M.A. was planning to celebrate its fifth anniversary on a cruise which departed from a port in Florida. A dear lady who lived in that state called the prayer line several times a month with her prayer needs, and the Lord impressed upon me that the anniversary celebration was the perfect opportunity to meet her in person and extend some much needed encouragement to her. At first, she thought it was some type of scam to be invited to join us on the cruise as our special guest, but as she sailed with us for a week, we showered her with love. Only her cabin mate and R.H.E.M.A.'s leadership team knew she was a special guest until she thanked us for the love shown to her, calling me "God's trophy of grace." A recent note from her read, "My friend, my sister, I just want you to know, outside of God, my children, and life, you are the best thing that could have ever happened to me! Forever is a long time, and that's how long I'll love you!" Now that I am no longer working at Family Life Radio, we still stay in touch.

As an influencer, it is also vital to be a servant leader. Position yourself to motivate and to understand what is important to the other person so that you will know how to go about getting the best out of them. Again, if there is something they are trying to achieve, affirm them and recognize their achievement. Remember, it is more about them than you. Hospital chaplains are occasionally on call for "end of life situations." One evening, I received a call from the hospital operator asking me to come to the hospital because a family was requesting a chaplain for their elderly mother, Mrs. Lee, who was expected to pass away that evening. As I entered Mrs. Lee's room in the intensive care unit (ICU), her tearful son, Ralph, thanked me for coming. Mrs. Lee was on life-support, but I asked Ralph if I could pray with him and his mother. He agreed—but he also told me that he had a lot of family in the ICU waiting room, and he was more concerned about the fact that he did not know if they believed in Jesus. He wanted me to go into the ICU waiting room and talk to his family about Christ. I understood and acknowledged his love for his family, and I thank God that Ralph's family was receptive to what I shared with them about Jesus. As I prepared to depart, I observed that Ralph's whole demeanor had changed. He gave me a quick smile as he thanked me again for coming. Shortly after my departure, I learned that Mrs. Lee had passed away.

To be a great influencer, I believe you need to be dependent on something powerful. For me, it's my dependence on God. I know I can't do anything in my own strength. Based on that, I can better understand my strengths and my weaknesses, take advantage of opportunities, and recognize obstacles or threats. My longtime friend, Mary, loved to go to the Ada S. Niles Senior Activity Center in Chicago every weekday as if she were going to work. One morning, Mary asked me to accompany her to the center even though I was too young to be a member. Upon arriving, she introduced me to Denise, the director of the center. Denise was quite cordial and directly asked, "Did you come to volunteer?"

Not wanting to say "no," I responded, "What do you need help with?"

She instantly replied, "I need someone who can run this center so I can take a day off sometimes."

Denise had never met me before that day, but I suspect Mary had been talking to her about me. I knew that Mary loved me and considered me a dear friend. Even though I had no experience working with seniors, I did not doubt that I could do the job. With over 30 years in management in the corporate world, my leadership skills had been tried, tested, and, with the help of God, proven too many times to mention. "I have to pray about it," I told her.

About two weeks had passed when God reminded me that my daughter Heather was getting married and Leroy and I had a wedding to pay for. The offer from Denise at the senior center was Him providing me an opportunity to meet that financial need and be active in the community. I acknowledged the challenge of interacting with a totally senior population, most of whom were set in their ways. Although I knew each day would be a unique experience, I truly believed that respect for me would follow if I prayed for wisdom and listened attentively, seeking to understand and address their individual and collective needs. It became one of the most rewarding jobs of my life.

In addition, seek to develop effective listening skills to best understand others, and great verbal skills so you can collect key pieces of information on what is important to your client. Ask yourself, "What do I need to do to please them?" "What are their goals and dreams and the relationships in their lives that might impact how well I influence them?" Great influencers develop relationships. That starts with knowing your own goals and the goals of whoever you are working with. You also need to understand your temperament, manage it, and be aware of the other person's temperament to best discern how that affects their behavior and yours.

As an influencer, it's essential to know the environment and culture you are in. Pursue objective actions and conversations, not with the motivation to impress, but to gain allies. This will allow you to build people as you influence them. In early 2013, my husband and I decided to transition from a traditional black Baptist church, located 45 minutes from our home, to a non-denominational church five minutes from home. We had worshiped and served in an African American church culture our entire lives, so the worship and sermon delivery in the non-denominational church was quite reserved from what we were used to.

Our first visit to the church was on its second anniversary, which was being celebrated by all of the members gathering in the courtyard for a fellowship luncheon. The members were cordial and welcoming, and the doctrine was Bible-based, so it was not long before this new cultural experience seemed normal to us. I was an ordained minister and had overseen the prayer and marriage ministry at our former church, but we came to the new church not knowing how our gifts, talents, and abilities would be used. Believing that God would make room for them in His way and timing, I faithfully participated in Sunday school, discipleship mentoring, women's ministry, and life group. When the existing prayer ministry leader had a desire to transition to lead the discipleship program, he recommended me to the church leadership to become the leader of the prayer ministry team.

I was granted permission for the church to begin meeting for prayer, and I subsequently started a weekly prayer conference call. The goal was to provide a way for people to get comfortable with praying out loud or in public. God has mightily blessed our prayer call, and participants are accepting the challenge of leading the call as well as praying aloud. I am encouraged because God has shown all of us that small steps bear fruit. The participants on the call truly believe in the power of prayer, and I can hear their increasing confidence as they pray. My husband and I are now also facilitating marriage enrichment workshops and premarital counseling when requested at the church.

We are all born with an innate sense of right and wrong, good and evil, but society also provides rules and laws that give us do's and don'ts for daily living. On top of that, we each have our own distinct personalities, abilities, likes, and dislikes. As we mature and age, there are also numerous influences from our environment, education, parents, teachers, and friends that impact the direction of our lives. All of these factors serve to inform how we influence others through our lives. I encourage you to look for ways to use your morals, gifts, and experiences to be an influencer. As you do, you'll be rewarded with joy—that sense that your life is making a difference and that you are making a contribution to society and helping someone else to achieve their goals.

So, where will my "quiet storm" take me next? I believe my future is found in building other influencers; specifically, helping people who have low self-esteem see that they have value, worth, skills, abilities, and talents that are useful. I want them to know that they, too, can receive joy because of how they can add value to others as they influence them.

JoAnn Johnson is an ordained minister, certified hospital chaplain, and a marriage enrichment coach and leadership trainer. She has over 30 years of experience in project/process management and consulting for communications corporations and in the religious community. She is founder/overseer of Retired Heroines Ever Magnifying the Almighty, Inc. (R.H.E.M.A.), a women's movement that builds disciple-makers for Christ, and she is founder of Awesome Daughters of R.H.E.M.A. (ADOR) whose members are provided resources on how to live victorious, godly lives. Contact JoAnn at rhemainformation@gmail.com

4

Delivering Your Best

Henry A. Kelly

DELIVERING PACKAGES IS pretty simple. You get a package. You put it on a truck. You take it to where it is supposed to go, deliver the package, and leave.

In practice, delivering influence may not be so simple—but I've learned that the principles behind being an influencer really aren't all that complicated. In the end, it's all about delivering your best to someone else so that everyone benefits.

My company, First Touch Logistics, is a delivery partner for a large logistics company in Atlanta, Georgia. I started the business in May 2019 with eight routes, eight vehicles, and 20 people. By mid-2020, we were running up to 50 routes per day with as many as 150 people working those routes. First Touch Logistics came about after I retired from a 32-year corporate career, all for the same company. I started in accounting for a decade before I began working in other departments from operations to marketing to external affairs, the latter of which afforded me opportunities to establish relationships with key customers including elected officials. My last role was as director of corporate relations, interacting directly with different constituents and customers.

After being retired for a couple of years, I had a desire to obtain my own business, so I started looking around and discovered the large logistics company I now serve. Being in a financially conservative situation, it made the most sense because the level of risk was not as high as other business models. The online shopping and delivery marketplace had blossomed in a big way over the last several years, and I felt I was in a position to take advantage of that.

I view influence from the context of engaging with an individual in a way that allows me to have the kind of relationship where I can discuss a situation, or a need that I have, and influence their behavior, thoughts, or actions. It's a relationship that garners huge credibility with that individual—one where they trust me and believe what I say is true.

During my corporate career, I was often in a position to impact an elected official, or a regulator, on a decision that would have an effect on our business. Through that, I gained experience, became more astute to what influence meant and how to deliver it, and then applied those insights to First Touch Logistics. The idea behind the name of our company is that we are the "first touch" for that package going out to the customer. Therefore, I needed to recruit, assemble, and develop a team of drivers who would be diligent, committed, perform their job safely, and take pride in their work. I believe one of my strengths is building relationships with people, and I wanted to position those who worked for First Touch to go on to bigger and better opportunities by having a good experience and building a track record of success.

The challenge was to build a connection among my team

at First Touch even though they all work independently. Once they pick up their packages for their route, they are on their own. To create a level of commitment for them to do the right thing during the course of each day, I believed it was essential to build a relationship with them as a company leader and influencer by doing right by them as far as their pay was concerned, making things easier for them by providing the resources they needed to be successful, providing rewards and recognition of their accomplishments, and trying to be responsive to their questions while making it an enjoyable place to work. If I succeeded, my team would have a degree of loyalty to the company, and therefore, want to do right by the company because the company was doing right by them. Unfortunately, our drivers don't always show up for work on their assigned days, especially when there's bad weather. One of the worst things that can happen in this type of business is not fulfilling route commitments, resulting in late deliveries. So, on one of those days that a driver calls out, the first thing I do is start calling drivers who are off to see if they can come in. One time, I called a driver who had already worked 30 hours over three consecutive days. I explained the situation to him, then asked, "Can you cover that route today?" Even though he had already made plans with his family, he agreed to reschedule them and come in because I had personally called him, and he wanted the company to be successful.

First Touch is graded by the large logistics company on a weekly basis and all of our drivers are rated, so the top five drivers each week are given a financial bonus. In addition, I started taking a route each year on my birthday, and each driver who completes all of their deliveries with excellence and beats me back to the warehouse will get a personal gift from me. Influence is predicated on relationship—and influence increases and is more effective and better received based on the quality of the relationship built around it. I'm not just giving my workers a job to do. I am striving to create a relationship where I am influencing them, and therefore, they are enabled to influence me. An obvious byproduct of this is that there is a positive influence on the customer, even though my employees may never actually meet them other than briefly at the front door. This makes our company successful. Dealing with the COVID-19 pandemic in 2020 was a tremendous challenge. Many individuals were required to shelter in place for months with many of their basic needs met only through home delivery. Often, our drivers made deliveries to the same home multiple times each week. Because of our drivers' dedication to ensure that people received their orders, we saw customers show their appreciation through everything from "thank you" signs and gift baskets to snacks and cool drinks left out on the front porch. Even though the customers and the drivers never met, there was an implied relationship that was established and honored.

I grew up in a blue-collar family in Augusta, Georgia, and my father, Thomas, had a significant influence on me. Family was always first, and he read the Bible and talked about the stories in Scripture and how they related to life. I grew up with a high level of respect for my father because he always did the right thing. He also worked for a corporation for nearly 30 years as a truck driver, and while he did not finish high school because he had to go to work to make ends meet for his family, he was a self-educated man who was great with his hands and could fix almost everything. My father did second-hand jobs doing various projects on other people's houses, and he demonstrated a high work ethic.

Dad didn't use a lot of words with me. I was the youngest of four, and my siblings were eight, 10, and 16 years older than me. I like to say I was the last good seed, in that my parents thought they were through having children when I came along. I grew up much like an only child. What I didn't realize as a youngster was how much my dad was a leader and influencer. He was a deacon in church and a member of a men's association where he had leadership roles. When there were challenging issues in the church, people sought him out for advice. They saw him as a straight shooter who also thought things through. That was a huge influence on how I managed myself. He also had leadership positions in the union of the company where he worked. I really didn't pay attention to what all of that meant when I was growing up, but I did later in life.

My dad was a quiet influencer, meaning that he didn't look to be the center of attention, but instead provided sound advice and guidance. My only son, Philip, and I were talking to my father one day when Philip was about 16 years old. As a teenager, Philip really didn't want to listen to much anything I had to say at that time. He felt he had all the answers. As my dad started to ask him questions about his future, it was obvious that Philip was all over the place with his thoughts. After listening to my son, my father began to tell him about his own youthful days, sharing a story about his aspirations when growing up and how limited they were in the deep south. My dad had to drop out of grade school to go to work so he could assist in supporting his family. At a point in the conversation, he raised his hands and said to Philip, "These are what I had to use to make a living. It was my only option!" He then pointed to his head and said, "But you have the option to develop and use your mind by taking advantage of education that can lead you to a quality of life that would exceed mine and could exceed your dads." Those few words influenced Philip to become a better student—and my son went on to college to get a business degree.

I remained in Augusta through college. My parents couldn't afford to pay for school, and I did not want to go away to college and incur the debt of a student loan. My parents said I could stay with them rent free as long as I paid for school, so I went to a local community college and worked my way through school. I had a part-time job the entire time I attended Augusta University, and I benefited from a co-op opportunity where I was paid to work in the accounting department of a company one semester on (working) and one semester off (in school). That school turned out to be a really good experience for me because I got involved in other things besides academics, and I really found my voice as a thoughtful adult. I joined the business club there and gained some leadership experience. I got involved in the Student Government Association (SGA), an organization responsible for governing student interests, advocating for their concerns, providing support for recognized student organizations, and serving students by hosting activities and events that enhance their lives. All of it gave me a foundational appreciation for building relationships with people.

I got to know one particular business professor quite well by regularly seeing him during his office hours. He recommended that I join the business club, which later led to a committee assignment within SGA. That committee was campus entertainment. What a stroke of genius, I thought, because our role was a fun one: selecting entertainers to perform on campus. The committee assignment even came with a budget and backstage passes! During my time on that committee, I got to take my very first airplane ride and attend my first convention where all types of entertainment options for college campuses were on display and we could book talent—a ventriloquist, comedian, juggler, or bands—for next year's school calendar. It gave me my one and only visit to San Antonio, Texas, where we toured the Alamo as part of our stay. We were making real decisions and representing the entire student body. I had a lot of fun and built a ton of self-confidence.

Another person who influenced me after I began working was named Jackie. I went into a department at the company called Accounting Research that was more of a think tank environment. The group took unique and different transactions and figured out how to best account for them based on the rules of accounting. Jackie was an African American, highly intelligent, a math major, and he knew his stuff. When it came to deep theoretical discussions, he was like a sage. I was a young African American male fresh out of college coming into an environment that was different and could be intimidating. Jackie showed me how a person could be good at what they did and command a level of respect so that people would come to him, asking for his opinions. He told me, "Hey, you can be good and be respected and be a brother." I'll never forget when Jackie invited me to attend a meeting with our company's board of directors' audit committee. The committee members were comprised of a subset of the board of directors who generally had a financial background and were leaders or audit partners at large Fortune 500 companies or public accounting firms. Jackie's presentation centered on the adoption of new accounting rules that would have a material impact on the company's financial statements. With a great deal of confidence and poise, Jackie delivered a concise and meaningful presentation, answering a barrage of questions without blinking an eye. To this day, I remember how proud and impressed I was as he commanded that room filled with powerful people. My takeaway from that experience is that knowledge is a powerful tool to exert influence in any setting.

There are three critical aspects to being successful as a person of influence. First and foremost, individuals have to trust you. They must have the confidence that you are the type of person who doesn't have a hidden agenda. You are to be very transparent in how you interact with them and be an honest person with honest intent. One common occurrence on boards of directors is a multitude of opinions on issues requiring board action. I served as vice chair on a not-for-profit board that was at a major crossroads from a funding perspective. Based on our mission, we found ourselves competing for funds in a crowded space with other organizations. One day, I recommended to the board chairman that we approach another organization that had a similar mission to ours and begin talks about a potential merger.

"You are the incoming chair in about a year," he replied.

"Why would you want to potentially eliminate the opportunity to be in that leadership position?"

"This is about the good of the organization," I told him, "not a personal agenda. In fact, if we don't consider something significant to address our fundraising, the organization might have to go out of business."

Ultimately, we moved forward with the merger, and it benefitted both organizations. The new board was comprised of representatives from both boards, and I was among those who didn't make it to the new board. But that was fine with me because the new organization was stronger and could contribute to the continuation of the mission, and that was most important.

Secondly, there has to be a level of mutual respect where you genuinely value the relationship that you have with them and are not just in it in pursuit of an outcome. In one of my roles during my corporate career, I was responsible for large commercial accounts like Walmart and Home Depot. My job was to assist those retail customers in being able to easily do business with my company. Often, we had to deal with conflicting internal policies across state lines that adversely affected these large businesses. During one such situation, I worked with attorneys in Georgia and Alabama who had different perspectives on how contract language would impact customers. Similar language was needed even though the stores were in different states. I had to use my influence to convince both attorneys to accept revisions to their original documents. My ability to gain their trust was essential, and I did it by respecting their individual positions on the matter and not make light of them. I achieved success by showing how we could demonstrate the needs of the customer as being superior to our own self-interests in a way where each party could accept some changes to their standard policies. As I was able to convince them the customer needs to be our first priority, we achieved success.

Lastly is listening. You build trust and mutual respect by being genuinely interested in what the other person has to say. Pay attention to what is important to them and to their value system. Hear who is important to them and discover the relationships they have with folks who you might have to interact with, such as a secretary. To best influence the individual with whom you are working, you might want to identify one or two people in their inner circle for the purpose of building a relationship with them. I found this paramount when working with elected officials who rely heavily on their staff to give them advice and input on their decisions. Secretaries of elected officials have tremendous influence. I remember Mary, who was the secretary for an elected official who had been in office for several years. An important vote was ahead, and our company was concerned about some key issues to be decided by that vote. Our desire was to secure the final appointment on the calendar with the elected official the day before the vote. Based on my relationship with Mary, she made sure that we had that spot reserved a week in advance. This was before today's pervasive use of texting and emails to do such things. Her ability to get us on the schedule gave us a chance to tell our story one more time, and ours was the last voice he heard before making his decision. The vote worked out in our favor.

In addition, you want to be humble as an influencer. You can be a quiet influencer who doesn't seek attention or recognition but is comfortable in your own skin. You know your strengths and your weaknesses, and you live by that old adage, "To thine own self be true." As an influencer, you need to be willing to let someone else get the credit. When dealing with elected officials, their focus is on serving their constituents and getting re-elected, so your best opportunity to establish a great relationship with an elected official comes by helping them solve an issue for their constituents. During one such situation, my company owned a plot of land and had torn down a structure that was on that property. The community wanted the land donated for development and pressured elected officials to make that happen. However, based on our prior use of the land, my company did not want commercial development on the property. We proposed to the elected official the idea of designating the land as "green space" so that it could be used as a community garden. The elected official loved the idea, and we allowed her to pitch the idea to the community as her own. It turned out to be a hit with everyone. The elected official was viewed as a hero, and we had a stronger relationship with her and the community.

The benefit of being a good influencer is that you are ultimately able to accomplish an objective or a goal. I am a competitive guy. I grew up playing football, and that is my favorite sport, but I like all sports. Today, golf allows me to enjoy some of that competitive nature even though I am older, and I am competing as much against the course as I am another person. If you are goal oriented, being an influencer can positively engage your competitive nature as you help yourself and others achieve their goals.

As I continue with First Touch Logistics, my hope is that as our workforce grows, I will have the opportunity to influence a younger generation of folks who can go on and have an impact on their families and their communities for the better—that a few of my life lessons can be shared and used to help with them in their life journey. Again, it all comes back to delivering your best, and there's no better way to be all you can be, and leave an impact on the lives of others, than through being an influencer.

Henry A. Kelly is a Certified Public Accountant and former Atlanta, Georgia corporate executive with more than 30 years of experience working numerous leadership positions that touched on nearly every aspect of the utility industry. He often acted as a change agent, charged by executive leadership with creating and implementing key strategic visions to enhance business and community engagement. Henry fulfilled a lifelong dream of becoming an entrepreneur by starting First Touch Logistics in 2019. He remains active in the community, including a term as chairman and president of 100 Black Men of Atlanta, Inc., an organization focused on financially supporting first generation African-Americans seeking a college education. Contact Henry at henryakelly@yahoo.com

5

Rooted in Love

Rosalind Longmire

THOSE WHO INFLUENCE others are true to themselves and don't try to get people to think like them. They accept others for who they are and where they are at that very moment.

I think of Antoinette Tuff. When a young man armed with an AK-47-type weapon came into the front office of the Ronald E. McNair Discovery Learning Academy outside Atlanta, Georgia in 2013, Antoinette calmly shared her deepest personal struggles, told the gunman she loved him, and even offered to walk outside with him to surrender so the police wouldn't harm him.[1] In the end, the suspect, Michael Brandon Hill, was taken into custody, and no one inside or outside the school was hurt. Today, Antoinette is a motivational speaker and author who, on her website, declares, "In a climate of political unrest, global health concerns, polarizing disagreements, and mental health crisis, psychological safety has become more important than ever. Together, we can take steps to problem solve, find common ground, and promote inclusive relationships."[2]

Then and now, Antoinette shows how communication is a key skill for an influencer. She had the attitude to care about Michael that fateful day at the school and lead him in a positive direction, and she's doing the same thing for others today.

Influence is a wonderful thing—and I believe it is rooted in love.

I am known in my home community of Tucson, Arizona as "the pastor of love." My very first sermon at Phillips Chapel CME, from John 4, was based on that very subject. Whether it has been as a successful businessperson as a licensed cosmetologist, or as pastor at the church where I grew up, I've always loved people. I want to see good and great things happen for humankind, and I seek to bring harmony and unity to all those I influence.

That is who I am. It is my passion.

Influence is the ability to have an impact on the conduct, nature, or character of a person or an organization to help them grow and reach a desired outcome. I have influenced others to excel, rise higher, and enhance themselves, especially in their spiritual lives, so they can move forward. I worked with one woman who wasn't where she wanted to be spiritually. She was a Christian, but she desired to become closer to God and solidify her prayer life and her relationship with Him. I applied what I learned as a child from my maternal grandmother, Lena Brown, when she lived with us and took care of me and my two older sisters while my parents were at work. I heard her praying throughout the day, and she was always quoting Scripture to us, putting it in everyday terms we could understand. Without fail, she had a time of prayer every morning and stopped to read her Bible three times a day. The Word was like a meal to her, and she loved to feed on its truth. So, I walked the woman through what Grandmother Lena did, and as a result of her example, what I do, encouraging her to have more frequent conversations with God. I suggested that she speak with the Lord as a friend, not an object, really communing with Him and talking with Him as if He were sitting in the room next to her. She began to read more Scripture and ask more questions about it, and it caused her to attend Bible study more often. She was able to grow in her relationship with God.

I also believe I have added value to others by being authentic to who God created me to be and by being transparent with them. When I was younger, I was crass with people. I was flippant with my mouth and said things that I probably shouldn't have. Right after I was out of high school, I got suspended from a job at a manufacturing company for telling a lady that I was going to "pray" for her. We'd had a disagreement, I was being quite sarcastic in the way I said it, and it was inappropriate. I'll take an example like that and share with others how God has tamed me so that I don't use that tone any longer. Through being transparent, I show people that I don't always get things right and I'm not afraid to acknowledge it. You are authentic when you tell others the truth about yourself.

As I've influenced others, I've learned three valuable lessons. First, you can achieve what you believe if you desire it. Six years after I had received my credentials as a pastor, I wanted to earn a clinical pastoral education certificate, knowing it would be good for me and would help me with my counseling assignments as a pastor. Sadly, a lot of things happened during my course work that overwhelmed me. My father got sick and passed away, then, toward the close of my studies, my brother-in-law died as well. More than once, I asked myself, "Do I stop, deal with these things that I am going through, and try again later, or do I just continue and do the best that I can?" Every time, my mindset was firm. "I want to complete this." So, I did—and to this day, I feel like it was a good decision. In fact, I desire to get even more certifications.

Second, you can improve where you are and make it better. Before becoming pastor at Phillips Chapel, I became an administrator there. The church had seen pastors come and go over the years. Records about the church's history, outreach, and organization were not kept as well as they could've been. I came in and fixed that, hearing the voices of my fellow congregants, listening to their concerns, and taking those issues into consideration in the process. I made a positive change that benefitted our entire church community, and made an influence that eventually led to me being named the pastor in 2010.

Third, if you don't like your present situation, you can transform it by thinking differently about it. I had weight issues over most of my life, and it wasn't until I changed my mindset, and became more diligent about exercise and eating, that I was able to bring myself to the healthier place I maintain today. I had to give up fad diets and workouts and make healthy living a lifestyle. I made significant changes, and others saw what I did and made changes in their lives as a result.

Among those who have significantly influenced me are two of my previous pastors. One, along with his wife, was pivotal to my decision not to get married many years ago. They helped me recognize that I was reaching for something that really wasn't there out of fear of never being married and becoming an old maid. I wanted to be a wife and a mother, and at 34 years of age, I saw that wasn't happening, and it scared me. Thanks to their counsel, I later married Al, God's chosen man for me.

The other pastor helped me to recognize the giftings God had given me and encouraged me to pursue His calling for my life. The process was difficult and sometimes hurt me to the point of tears, but it was essential for me to know that I was not done, there were still more things to do, and that God had something amazing ahead for me if I just continued to believe. That helped me to do what I am today as a pastor who loves people regardless of where they are in life. In their own ways, both pastors encouraged me in my spiritual walk, my calling, and my giftings, pulling out what they saw in me that I sometimes didn't see in myself. They pushed me forward and built my confidence to be able to do whatever it was that I put my mind to.

In addition, others have influenced me regarding what to do as well as what not to do. I was a shy kid who mostly kept to myself. I was a good student, but I didn't have a lot of friends throughout elementary and middle school because everyone saw me as being a "holy roller." I wasn't out late at night or getting into trouble, and I also wasn't interested in some of the things they were doing. It's not like I carried my Bible around or anything, but they knew I went to church. I didn't want them to call me "holy roller" because I thought it was negative. It wasn't until high school, after I joined the track team my sophomore year, that I attained a level of popularity with my peers. My track coach, Marisella Kitt, was inspirational to me. She told me, "There is something in you that is not like the other girls." Mrs. Kitt told us to keep our heads up high and believe in ourselves. She also helped me to feel better about myself and to realize that I was not so different from everybody else just because of my faith and the fact that I enjoyed some things they didn't. With her influence, I came out of my shell and started the journey to become the person I am today.

Developing a vision about how you can influence others is vital. Proverbs 29:18 tells us that where there is no vision, the people perish. You have to look forward and have hope. There is something greater *for* you. There is something greater *in* you. Look beyond the circumstances that you see and imagine what is possible—and that's how you can discover how you can be an influencer.

If you desire to become an influencer, or increase your established impact as an influencer, strive to be a leader who is genuine, honest, kind, and able to listen to others and respect their opinion. If you are also flexible and open, you can influence in different situations because every situation is different and unique to the person or organization. Once, a couple came to my office and told me about the difficulties they were having because of the husband's addiction to gambling. I was eager to help them, but with one stipulation: that they look at getting some professional help for the gambling addiction. They agreed, and as I worked with them, I realized that when people come with that kind of situation and the pain it causes, I need to love them into their healing. Therefore, I didn't scold. I didn't give a sermon on the evils of gambling. I didn't ridicule them or do anything to make them feel unworthy or less than other couples. I just loved them through. In the end, they resolved their issues and he stopped gambling just before his death.

To develop your abilities as an influencer, you can learn from others who have influenced you, but I also think there is a natural instinct within you to have an influence. If you are a believer in God, the power of the Holy Spirit lives in you and influences that instinct. That instinct served me well when a young woman came to me to discuss the relationship problems she was having with her mother. The woman was not married, and her mom did not approve of her lifestyle. The mother was a Christian who had tried to raise her children as best she could in a church environment, but the daughter said her mom constantly condemned her lifestyle. She wanted to have a relationship with her mother, but the friction and tension between them was too much.

I listened to the woman, informed her that her choice wasn't a lifestyle that I would choose, but if she wanted a relationship with her mother, she had to respect her mother's point of view whether she agreed with it or not. "That is an issue that you'll really have to take up with God," I counseled.

As I then asked her about her prayer life and about reading the Word of God, I felt the Holy Spirit tell me, "Don't condemn her. Just point her to my Word. Plant the seed, and somebody else will come behind you and water it." Today, she talks about her relationship with God more often, and I believe in the Spirit's directive that another person will come into her life perfectly equipped to help her. The woman and her mother reconciled, and she has ended up taking care of her mother's needs and visiting her regularly after her mother was diagnosed with dementia.

The rewards of being an influencer are building relationships with others, seeing their self-esteem and self-worth grow, and watching them blossom like butterflies and flow through life. I'm convinced that as long as you have breath in your body, you can still influence people and have a positive impact. You can also see future generations move forward because of what they've learned from you, even as you learn from them.

Rosalind Longmire is pastor of Phillips Chapel CME Church, the church where she has served all of her life, and she is also a licensed cosmetologist. Her heart's desire is to allow God to use her to build His Kingdom through loving, serving others, teaching, and preaching the Gospel of Jesus Christ. Contact Rosalind at rozlong52@aol.com

Notes

1 "Antoinette Tuff hailed as 'true hero' for handling Georgia school gunman," by Greg Botelho, Vivian Kuo, and Josh Levs, CNN, Thursday, August 22, 2013. https://www.cnn.com/2013/08/21/us/georgia-school-gunshots/index.html

2 https://antoinettetuff.com/

6

Untapping Your Potential

Dr. Claudette Owens

IF YOU SEND me an email, when I respond, you'll notice a tag line at the end of the communication: "Character defines you. Thoughts shape you. Initiative carries you. God blesses and keeps you."

That's my personal mission statement. The character we have is who we are, especially our trustworthiness and honesty. When it comes to our thoughts, if we think positively, we will usually have a positive outcome. Yet if the ultimate outcome is not as positive as we hoped, a positive attitude can help us understand that it still worked out for our good. With initiative, I have found that most of the promotions I have received over the years resulted from the small things no one else took the initiative to do, but I did. Finally, how God blesses and keeps us is self-explanatory. If we do all these other things, the Lord has promised to bless us, particularly when we keep His commandments.

God has certainly blessed me. Quantus Link, LLC is my consulting company. It was originally founded in 2002 as Bethel Development, LLC. My husband, Edward, and I flipped houses until the stock market crash in 2008. Since the structure was already in place, I then started consulting under that structure. Today, I do personal consultations and professional development with local companies, universities, and community organizations in various technical areas such as cybersecurity, document reviews, and proposal reviews, preparation, workshops, and training. I have bachelor's degrees in electrical engineering from the University of Alabama at Huntsville and in electrical engineering technology from Alabama A&M University. I also have a master's degree and a doctorate in physics from Alabama A&M. It was the latter that served to confirm my belief in God. The knowledge of my faith was further developed with a doctorate in ministry, master's degrees in divinity and biblical studies, and my ongoing work with the non-profit organization, Fountain of Life Ministries. There, I partner with other non-profits in the North Alabama community that support youth, senior citizens, and veterans, provide scholarships, and administer summer youth camps.

Yet it's not any of those achievements, as wonderful as they are, that have made me an influencer. Rather, it is my passion for people and my desire to see each one bring out the greatness inside of them that propels me forward to impact others. There is so much untapped potential inside every one of us. When something is untapped, it simply means it has potential that has not yet been fully realized. An untapped resource is something valuable that has not yet been taken advantage of or used. We don't really understand or know what we have, but I like to say, "Nobody can be better at being you than you."

I was reminded of that truth when I was contacted a few years back by my high school graduation classmates from 1979, saying that someone should schedule a class reunion. When I told them that I'd attend if someone put it together, one of them, Dennis, replied, "You are the class president."

"No," I responded, "I was never a class officer the entire four years we were in high school."

He said, "Well, we always thought it was you because you were so bossy, and we always did what you told us to do. We thought it was you."

Now, I prefer not to think that I'm "bossy," but I take that as an indication of how I'm an influencer. Looking back over my life, even when I was an entry level employee, when I have shared ideas, wisdom, or guidance, others have told me, "That is good," or "I should try that." Accordingly, I have been blessed to mentor up to 20 individuals over my career. We've talked about suggestions for their careers, and they have followed them. Some now work in cybersecurity. Others have gone on to get master's degrees or doctorates. A few are senior executives. One of my first mentees was Fredrick, a bright and intelligent mechanical engineering HBCU (Historically Black Colleges and Universities) graduate. He was well dressed, well spoken, and eager to learn, grow, and progress. But as we got to know each other, I kept hearing something. He'd talk about his desire to go to medical school. From that point on, we began to talk about his passion and the opportunities available to him. When a chance presented itself to get a master's degree in biomedical engineering, we talked about it, weighed the pros and cons, and looked at the other doors it would open.

Fredrick completed the program in about 18 months and

went on to medical school to become a surgeon. He still reaches out to me from time to time for advice. A recent correspondence from him said, "I was just thinking back to when we all worked together ... you often encouraged me to chase my dream of being a surgeon." I received his message on a day I was asking God about my legacy and why He'd directed me to retire from a very lucrative position. Often, we get so caught up in leaving an inheritance (the material things we leave behind) that we fail to think about legacy. Our legacy are the things we have imparted in people's lives in the "dash" between the two dates on our headstone to make an impact that reaches far beyond our death. Influence is key to leaving that legacy.

Influence is being able to move someone from where they are to another place using our inspiration, motivation, impact, and guidance. As the title of this book suggests, I believe influence is indeed ABC:

- A = Achievable (through teaching, learning, experience, and observation)
- B = Bestowed (in that some people are born with inherent qualities and traits of natural influence)
- But both must be:
- C = Cultivated (matured over time through perception, future training, growth, experience, and practice)

This became clear to me a few years back when I visited my hometown of Frisco City, Alabama for a family reunion. I was talking with one of my classmates, Dennis, who I mentioned previously, about old times, and he reminded me of the time when our teacher, Mrs. Lamar, asked each of us to actually teach a portion of her lesson that day. After I presented my part of the lesson, Dennis told me, "Claudette, you should be a teacher. I understood everything you said so clearly." As the years passed, I always seemed to be the go-to person in school—and that carried all the way through college and into my career. I realized that God had taken that and allowed me to (A) achieve influence through consultation and development that was (B) bestowed upon me naturally and that I had (C) cultivated through leadership training and experiences in college and beyond. I have influenced managers, senior level, and military leaders. Even now, I am adjusting to various cultural differences, technology influences, and fast-paced, instantaneous twenty-first century mindsets to mature and ensure I can continue to reach people where they are.

Another of the top characteristics of great influencers is being a good communicator who is reliable and discreet. Sometimes people are going to trust you with information you need to keep private, and it is easy to lose trust if you're not properly discreet. I've also discovered that if you are an influencer, you must have integrity. That is key because influence bestows *power*, and we have to be careful with the power with which we have been entrusted. As a pastor of worship arts and technology at my church, I know that counseling is a key area of influence in my ministry to others. The goal of counseling is to influence others to act, think, or move in a better or more positive direction. It gives me the power to influence a person's behavior and life. I've counseled numerous couples on the brink of divorce, young people trying to make life decisions, parents and children trying to handle the stresses of peer pressure, and men and women battling mental diseases and addictions. In these roles, influence is a power that must not be taken lightly.

Years ago, I counseled a woman I'll call Carol. She was struggling with so many things in her life but had a sincere desire to make a better life for herself. Whenever Carol experienced a success, she'd come to me and say, "Mrs. Claudette, I did it! I did it!" We celebrated together. If Carol felt she had failed, she'd start by saying, "Don't be mad at me, but—" Carol had a lot of negative influences pulling her toward the wrong things, including drugs and depression. Her existence was a roller coaster ride. One night, I received a call from Carol at 3:00 a.m. She was in a low place. I tried sharing Scripture with her. She said she didn't want to hear it. I tried praying. She said she was tired of prayers. "They aren't working. I just want to die."

For the next hour, nothing I said was right, and being a young mother at the time, my thoughts turned to having to get myself dressed, my children up and ready for school, and then going to work. Thinking about some "tough love" tips I'd recently read, I said, "Carol, you know that is not really what you want to do. You have so much of life ahead of you if you are just willing to go through the rehabilitation it takes to overcome this thing. I need to go now. I can't make up your mind for you. You must come to terms for yourself. Now try to get some sleep and call me tomorrow." Then I hung up.

I didn't realize the power of my words. Around 6:00 a.m., the phone rang again. I was certain it was Carol. Instead, it was one of her family members. "Can you get to the hospital as quickly as possible?" Carol had overdosed. My heart sank, and I started trembling. *What have I done?* I felt so guilty.

To God be the glory, Carol lived—and (I cry as I write this) Carol still trusted and needed me afterward. That was a life-altering moment for me. It changed everything about my approach to counseling. I dramatically realized the power that comes with influence—and it must be used with integrity, wisdom, and His guidance.

Influence is essential in leading others. Influencers know the importance of being someone who is trusted and respected, and they do whatever it takes to earn both. This commitment makes them a powerful role model for doing the right things the right way. Good influencers are often likeable, passionate, authentic, engaging, visible, and walk with authority. There are several ways to develop the skills of a person of influence: training, self-awareness, and tapping into what makes you who you are. Training can help develop some of these characteristics of influence, as well as listening to your mentors. Ask your mentor to make a checklist of key traits of influencers, then have your mentor ask you about those traits and do an evaluation of how well you demonstrate them. For example, your mentor can ask, "Do you listen well?" or "You may be a good motivator, but do you really hear what others say to you?"

In today's world, one's image seems to take center stage. We tend to make the voices of others more credible than the voice inside of us. Looking inside is one of the best ways to begin bringing out that greatness within you. One of my most treasured lifelong memories of tapping into my inner greatness came when I was at Frisco City High School. My best friend, Pam, asked me to try out for the cheerleading squad. I'd always loved cheering, and I knew I could lead the students to enthusiastically support the team. I also had the ability to do excellent jumps, splits, and cartwheels—but I had a problem. I did not have a cheerleader's body, or, at least, what had been defined as one. Because of issues with my weight, I did not see myself becoming a cheerleader.

Pam, however, would not take "no" for an answer, so, despite my reservations, I signed up for tryouts. I attended every practice, even though the other girls looked at me sideways, and some other students even taunted me. Pam always stood up for me and made sure the two of us practiced together and alone so that I could get everything down right.

Tryout day arrived, and with other students watching on, I was nervous but excited. When my name was called, I stepped up—and something seemed to come alive in me! Everything I was asked to do came easily, even the challenging round off cartwheel into a split. When I was finished, some of the same students who had taunted me were now cheering for me. I made the squad, cheered for the rest of my junior year, and the next year was awarded the highest score during tryouts. I also discovered a new area of influence, as my passion for cheering even resulted in fans from opposing teams coming up to tell me how much they enjoyed watching me cheer. There was some untapped potential in me that was brought out when I stopped allowing my weight problem to overshadow the greatness inside of me. In the end, cheering not only unlocked my potential, but it helped me control my weight problem.

My biggest fans have been in my corner from the very beginning. They are the people who have had the most influence in my life. It started with my parents, Osia and Inez Carmichael. I was adopted—and that's significant to me because they didn't have to bring me into their family. They chose to. In my case, my birth mother and my adoption mother are sisters. My birth mother had some challenges, so my parents decided to adopt me even though they couldn't afford it. They gave me their name and their life. Not only that, they also poured principles into me that still guide my life. My mom told me, "Always be honest and truthful. Always be open. Don't have people guessing if something bothers you. Don't backstab people. Always speak to them and always speak with respect." My dad constantly encouraged me to help people along the way. These different things have become a part of who I am.

Growing up in the 1960s-70s wasn't easy. We didn't have the opportunities that are afforded to young blacks today. I loved school, and I was always curious about how things worked. I had my heart set on being a scientist. But when I talked to my high school counselor about my aspirations, he said, "You are a very smart girl, but the best you can be is a secretary, possibly a nurse." I was hurt to my core. My principal met me in the hallway, and he could see I was upset. "Look me in my eyes," he said. "The only person that can stop you from being who you want to be is you." That helped so much. Still, later at the dinner table, my parents knew something was wrong. As I told them what the counselor said, I began to cry. I felt so belittled. It was the first time I realized the world had a different view for me because of my race and gender.

That night I got what we in the African American community call "the talk"—about how I needed to act and respond different to others because I was a black woman. My parents told me I'd have to work twice as hard just to be on the same page with my counterparts. They instilled within me the importance of a good work ethic and of taking initiative. They reiterated what my principal said and reminded me that I could be anything I wanted to be if I worked hard to achieve it. The final thing I remember about that night was them putting their arms around me and telling me how much they loved me.

A lot of people say I act just like my parents—and for me, that is a compliment.

After my parents, my two other biggest influencers were the first two bosses I had in my career. One, Sarah Jamar, was when I was an intern working in the TOW Missile Product Assurance Office at the Redstone Arsenal United States Army post near Huntsville, Alabama. An African American female, Sarah showed me four principles I needed to walk by as an African American woman by teaching me first to WADE:

- W = Work hard.
- A = Always be there.
- D = Don't wait to be asked.
- E = Eagerly ask if there is anything you can do and take initiative.

The other, Doyce Satterfield, a white male, was my first supervisor after I became a permanent civilian employee with the U.S. Army. He told me he saw something in me and declared three things over me. "Number one, you are going to be successful because I am going to help you. Number two, you are going to take my job. Number three, you are going to get a Ph.D." Eventually, I did take his position and then went a position above that. When I received my Ph.D., he and his wife were there to support me.

Both Sarah and Doyce instilled within me principles of professionalism and commitment, and they guarded and guided my career. They are still my mentors today, and when I had my retirement ceremony in 2018, I was honored and blessed to have them there and to be able to recognize them for their contributions to my life and my career.

One of my favorite responsibilities in my career was a summer internship program for one of the organizations I supported out of the office of the secretary of defense. I once ended up with two African American females who I'll call Shaunna and Yvonne. From different colleges and backgrounds, they were smart and anxious to learn—and I immediately saw an opportunity to give to them what my earlier mentors had given to me. These ladies had the skills and abilities, and I knew they would not have a problem learning the processes and technical initiatives we had planned for them. But I quickly identified some areas that would hinder them in the future.

So, I made it my personal responsibility to spend not just work time, but my own personal time, mentoring them in professional development. My team and I worked together to come up with a project that would benefit us but also match and enhance Shaunna's and Yvonne's skill sets. We worked on everything from the importance and value of time to professional dress and presentations, leading a meeting, and understanding the culture and expectations of corporate and military environments. Shaunna and Yvonne were required to present their work to leadership at the end of the summer at an internship conference. When they got up to present, they immediately got everyone's attention. Shaunna and Yvonne were dressed in black dress and pant suit attire with a single strand of pearls. The technical team had prepared them on how to present their project details, and they made eye contact with the audience members. They blew away both their peers and the leadership! After the conference, the office of the secretary of defense asked me to help them develop a standard development model for the internship program. It was a joy and privilege to do so.

At the time of my retirement, I was director for the Future Warfare Center. It was a geographically dispersed organization with about eight different locations, and I was the operations manager over all of them. When I took the job, my first goal was to see what I could do to bring everything into unity and make everyone feel important and a part of the organization. We took a new look at all of our processes, I sat with everyone and talked about that, and I took all of their concerns into consideration and reworked the processes from there.

When it was time to retire, they begged me not to go, but I didn't want to give them another year because God had assured me it was time. I remember I was surprised at God's direction. I had the support of every one of the employees and leadership, things were going right, and the money was coming through. I was on the mountaintop. When I asked God what I was supposed to do, He said He would show me, adding that previously it was about career, but now it was going to be about legacy—a chance to pour back into other people some of the things He had done for me.

It's so exciting! One of the things I am proud to be doing now is my service on the foundation board for the Alabama School of Cyber Technology and Engineering. Cybersecurity is my passion and being on the board allows me to impact young people. I was recently volunteering, reading to a kindergarten class and talking to them about being everything they could be. I asked the children, "Who can stop your dreams? No one can stop them. You are the only one."

As I look to the future, I am committed to staying focused and conscious of the needs and trends of the world and society around me. We live in a global, yet largely virtual and social media-driven, society where honesty, transparency, and equality are valued. Opinions and views are largely formed by the information received from social media, so our ability to connect quickly with people, be well informed, and win their trust is critical. People can and will tune us out or turn us off with just a click, and we may never get another opportunity to reach them.

As an influencer, I know I must understand people more, have a deep commitment to my own convictions, maintain integrity, and ensure that my personal goals and values are in alignment with the goals and values of the change I'm guiding others toward achieving. My reward from all of this is simple. Each time I see someone meet a goal, do something they never believed they could, or reach a point they never imagined, I see my legacy becoming a little more significant. I feel an unexplainable joy and gladness in my heart. For me, the rewards are more about them than about me. I made a difference in someone's life, and therefore I helped to change the world.

I want you to realize that you can influence at all levels. Influence is not positional, it is personal. You have opportunity to influence everyone: from your children and your neighbors to your spouse and those who work with you, including your supervisors. Don't hesitate to bring out the greatness within you to make a difference in the lives of others and build your legacy.

Dr. Claudette Owens is president and CEO at Quantus Link, LLC. She is also an author, speaker, preacher, and teacher with a passion for people. She has over 34 years of experience in space and missile defense support, leadership development, team building, mentoring, proposal evaluation, computer resources, networks, and communications, as well as information assurance, cybersecurity, and models and simulations. Contact Claudette at drclaudetteowens@gmail.com

7

On the Right Side of Changing the World

Dr. Yvette Rice

I BELIEVE THAT I am commissioned daily to assist someone in elevating their passion to fulfill their vision or purpose. Sometimes it is through sharing my knowledge or insight as a mentor. Other times it is as a coach, where I ask the right questions that lead others to do a self-assessment and decide on their next step forward. There are instances where I am a cheerleader who encourages someone along their journey. Whether it is in a two or three minute engagement or via an ongoing relationship where we meet on a weekly or monthly basis, I carry out my commission—and it is so fulfilling when people, especially young women professionals, just want to talk and share that I have impacted their lives.

That's influence, and it is a privilege to be an influencer in the lives of so many incredible individuals.

Influence is defined as the capacity to have an effect on the character, the development, or the behavior of someone or something. When I looked at that definition, these words just jumped off the page at me.

- Character.
- Development.
- Behavior.

My greatest passion in life is to add value to the lives of others from a developmental perspective, both professionally and personally, demonstrating the importance of character and integrity upon who they are and what they do. I choose to influence others by helping them become their best at who they were created to be—and be on the right side of changing their world.

That desire comes from being influenced so significantly by others. My home and my family are my first areas of influence, and my parents, my husband, and my children have impacted me in such an incredible way. I was raised in a middle-class family in Decatur, Alabama. Although my parents married right out of high school, they were hard working and lived a life of integrity. My father, Maurice, enlisted in the United States Army to take care of my mother who was expecting their first child. Even though Decatur was a blue-collar town, my mother, Annie, was determined to receive a formal education, purposing in her heart to become an educator. While working full-time, my mother not only earned her bachelor's degree as an educator, she also earned her master's degree between the late 1960s and early 1970s. My parents' determination influenced me and still does to this day, reminding me that I can succeed regardless of the obstacles I may encounter. My husband, Sam, was raised in a government housing project in Decatur, yet he graduated from Talladega College in 1974. He was the first in his family to get a degree, and he also became the first African American to be hired as a juvenile probation officer for Morgan County, Alabama. I always want to give back to my family the best of who God created me to be as a daughter, a wife, and a mother because they have always pushed me to grow as a human being.

Professionally, I have mentors and coaches who have thrust me, elevated me, and encouraged me to excel. Dr. Amanda H. Goodson has the ability to draw the very best out of anyone that she is around. I've watched how she has grown and the career she has developed in her life, and it inspires me. She has been a wonderful mentor and coach who has pushed me to want to develop even further. In my late fifties and early sixties, John Joseph IV, the executive director of the Decatur-Morgan County Entrepreneurial Center, became such a great leader, motivator, cheerleader, coach, and mentor. It was John who exhorted me, at 60 years of age, to get a master's degree in business administration through the Jack Welch Management Institute at Strayer University. The professors at Strayer have greatly influenced me, seeing and pulling out the best in me, whether it was through a challenging assignment or by asking questions to help me develop my critical thinking process.

I understand that, as one who influences others, I must grow. I need knowledge. I need wisdom. I need to see myself as a lifelong learner. While serving as the program manager for a government contractor, I realized that my team was experiencing some dysfunctionality. I also recognized that in order to bring the team together to successfully fulfill our contractual obligation, I needed to enhance my leadership skills, especially regarding team building. Initially, I enrolled in a leadership course related to understanding personality traits. I applied the knowledge I gained to better understand myself and my team. I discovered that, if a leader does not understand who they are from a personality perspective and know their strengths and weaknesses, they can't influence properly. Once those skills were developed, I enrolled in another online leadership development opportunity to further increase the tools in my leadership toolbox.

I am happy to say that our team began to function successfully, and even though I no longer work for that company, former teammates or employees that worked under me still keep in touch with me. When they have needed some guidance, wanted some inspiration, or were seeking to change their careers, they have contacted me to ask what my thoughts were about the situation or if I knew someone who could help them. It blesses me to know that not only did I add value in that organization and help them realize their strengths and how to be better teammates, but that those skill sets are still there. I am blessed to help them as they go forth today.

Finally, from a spiritual perspective, my greatest influence is my Lord and Savior, Jesus Christ, and the Word of God. Every aspect of elevating the lives of others can be found in the Bible. Matthew 5:13-16 tells us, "Let me tell you why you are here. You're here to be salt-seasoning that brings out the God-flavors of this earth. If you lose your saltiness, how will people taste godliness? You've lost your usefulness and will end up in the garbage. Here's another way to put it: You're here to be light, bringing out the God-colors in the world. God is not a secret to be kept. We're going public with this, as public as a city on a hill. If I make you light-bearers, you don't think I'm going to hide you under a bucket, do you? I'm putting you on a light stand. Now that I've put you there on a hilltop, on a light stand—shine! Keep open house; be generous with your lives. By opening up to others, you'll prompt people to open up with God, this generous Father in heaven." (MSG) Clearly, God's intent is that we positively influence others to live a life of purpose that is reflective of who we are as His children. God places us strategically in places of influence to create change, build hope, and encourage others who may not realize their importance or purpose on the earth.

As a minister who co-pastors a church with my husband, Bishop Sam Rice, Th.D., I will forever have gratitude for Dr. Karockas Watkins, the pastor who would not allow me to decline an invitation to come to his church and preach—an opportunity that spurred my development as a woman pastor and church leader. Karockas also introduced me to the need to develop myself as a leader, speaker, and coach.

As an influencer, I have the responsibility to shift the character, development, and behavior of an individual, and I am accountable to make sure that my motives are always pure. When I went through the John C. Maxwell online university in leadership, coaching, and development, John said leadership *is* influence—and that even though there are "born" leaders who have a natural ability to lead others, that ability still has to be nurtured and developed. Therefore, I'm convinced that anyone who is great at influencing can learn to be a great leader. Unfortunately, I have seen so many leaders who use their power to influence for the wrong reasons. They look to build themselves and their empires. Yet people are so hungry for someone to pour into them or pay attention to them, they can fall prey to influencers with selfish motives. That's why I realize that how I impact others is always to be to the betterment of others, not myself.

In addition, having the power to influence does not mean I have been given the authority to relive my life or duplicate myself through someone else's life. Each one of us has been given a unique fingerprint of gifts, abilities, and experiences. Therefore, our marks on the earth should be very different because each of us has an individual purpose. This valuable lesson was crucial for me as a parent. My husband and I have two beautiful children, Sharné and Samuel Christopher. Although they both chose a career path in science and engineering like me, their paths to fulfillment in life have been completely different from mine. Sharné was a math whiz from kindergarten all the way through high school, but she first considered becoming a pharmacist, then a pediatrician, before realizing on her own that neither field fulfilled her true desires. Ultimately, she chose to go to college and major in actuarial science, a discipline that applies mathematical and statistical methods to assess risk in insurance, finance, and other industries and professions. Upon graduation, Sharné went to work for the same company that employed me before she went to work for the United States Department of Defense and earned her master's degree in systems engineering. Samuel Christopher, meanwhile, showed his gifting early on as he took apart toys, put them back together, and played with building blocks as a little boy. He could build anything. Today, he is a manufacturing engineer in the automotive industry. Even my "daughter-in-love," Amber, changed her career field to engineering after realizing the opportunities for women in Science, Technology, Engineering and Mathematics (STEM) and observing all the female engineers in our family.

The Bible tells us to train our children in the way they should go (Proverbs 22:6). That doesn't mean we are to force them into anything, but direct them in the ways they are already gifted or talented. As parents, it's our responsibility to recognize the gifts that are already there and nurture them in our children so that they can develop into who they were created to be—and it's been my joy to influence my kids to fulfill their God-given destinies.

Regarding how I influence others, as a woman of faith, I am first accountable to God. The only way to maintain this accountability, especially if you are a person of faith, is to spend time in prayer, study the Word of God, and make sure that you are following the path that God has for your life so that you can be in the right place at the right time to meet, or engage with, that person you are supposed to influence. In addition to the Bible, I also believe you need to read books written by wonderful leaders such as Dr. Myles Munroe, Joyce Meyer, and Dr. Amanda H. Goodson who have empathy, compassion, and love for mankind. It is necessary for us to study those books—and for us to write books (like this one) that can encourage and influence one another positively. In order to be a responsible influencer, I am to exemplify characteristics of integrity, character, passion, and empathy. I also need to be able to put myself in the shoes of the other person.

There was a young woman who was part of an interracial congregation, and she was deeply hurt after her pastor had said some painful things regarding race relations. She called me and said she had been watching me and my husband teach and preach online. She was so broken she almost felt like giving up. I was able to encourage her and share Scripture with her, so she could hear God and make decisions that spoke to her heart. Sometimes God wants to push us forward as we are trying to hold on to a particular situation when, just like the disciples in the Bible, we are being told to go out and influence the whole world. It was persecution that forced the disciples out of the city and into the uttermost parts of the world, and the disappointment she felt at her church congregation forced her out of her comfort zone and into a whole new area of influence and growth in her life. God is now using her to influence change within that congregation.

As an influencer, I am to have wisdom and use my insight and understanding of an environment, or what the person's mission is in life, before I can influence them in any way. Finally, I must have faith in other people as well as faith in my own abilities. I'm convinced we are in a critical time on the earth. We are privileged to be here because each one of us is positioned to be a change agent if we are attentive, listening, and being where we are supposed to be. We have a choice to lose our own motives, be on the receiving end of something great, and become passionate, loving, and empathetic toward others—or we will end up missing the opportunity to influence in the right way. As a leader, I know my words have to be the right words for the right time because my words have power. They can build and heal, or they can destroy.

In the areas of engineering, program management, leadership and professional development, and technical writing, I aid others in being able to acquire businesses through opportunities—from writing proposals to empowering them to better prepare or serve their clientele with user documentation or training. I also use my team leadership strengths to assist organizations and individuals when they want to raise their levels of potential through curriculum development or leadership training. I have used both my abilities as a facilitator and engineer to influence technical leaders to help develop their skills in communication, leadership, or team building so they can shift the workplace culture to one where everyone can grow and is given a voice. In 2019, I did some training for an organization on conflict management. The company realized there are different modes for how to handle conflict, and out of their group of close to 20 people, there was not one individual who operated collaboratively, which meant that they didn't talk to each other when it came to problem solving and decision making. I had the opportunity to actually create a shift in that organization. I saw it as a privilege.

Being an influencer is sometimes all about networking and building relationships as you seek to meet the needs of the customer. The most important thing is to find out what the greatest need is. If I know I can't meet that need, I have to find someone who can. By providing for their need, even if I can't do it personally, I have planted a seed, and somewhere down the road I can reap a harvest when they remember how I went out of my way to help them. When I do this, I'm not giving away business. I am building a relationship. As I show others my integrity and character, they will come back to me. More than anything, I will win their business with trust. I always remember that people are watching me, no matter where I am or what I am doing. When my son was young, I was driving him and a group of elementary children to a field trip. Later, when one of the young ladies got home, she told her mother, "Mom, Mrs. Rice is something special. We were riding, and I watched her. Whatever the sign said that had the speed limit on it, that is what Mrs. Rice drove all the way there and all the way back."

When her mother told me that, it spoke volumes to me. If nothing else, I influenced that child to be a safe driver just by doing the right thing.

My reward from being an influencer all comes down to this: I just want to hear, "Well done, my good and faithful servant." (Matthew 25:21) I just want to be able to look into the lives of different people and think, "You know, God, thank you that you allowed me the privilege to be able to influence that person's life." As I look to the future, I'm convinced that the best is yet to come. I feel there is a shift coming in my career and my life, and I believe God will provide me a larger platform to influence others. I see it expanding.

As you consider how you can be an influencer, know that you have been put on this earth for a purpose. This is *your* time. If you seek to do the right thing, live with integrity, have a passion and empathy for others, and develop your leadership skills, your area of influence will increase.

Be on the right side of changing the world.

Dr. Yvette Rice is a results-oriented executive with front-end-of-the-business acumen and demonstrated success in the development and execution of technical communications strategies that maximize team effectiveness, develop talent, and drive lasting cultural change. A published author, Dr. Rice utilizes her 30 years of expertise, influence, and business insight to partner with senior executives of large corporations to produce books, white papers, and prolific articles related to leadership development, mentorship, coaching, as well as business advancement. A published author, Dr. Rice is also co-pastor with her husband, Bishop Sam Rice, Th.D., at New Genesis Community Church in Tanner, Alabama. Rice recognizes her purpose in life is to help others realize their true capabilities and maximize their potential. Contact Yvette at yvette.rice@llve-llc.com

8

The Powerful Responsibility of Influence

Catherine Ripley

"THE KEY TO successful leadership is influence, not authority," said author, speaker, and business consultant Kenneth H. Blanchard.

What do Taylor Swift, Dwayne Johnson, Nancy Pelosi, Mohamed Salah, and Sandra Oh have in common? They are a singer, pop icon, politician, athlete, and actress—and they were among the 100 people chosen in Time Magazine's "Most Influential People" in 2019. Celebrities hold a lot of power over the masses, and in our world of instant access to social media, their influence is global. That's a lot of power. The question is, how can we "non-celebrities" use our personal influence to make the world better?

Influence, by pure definition, is the ability to directly or indirectly affect another person to take action or make a decision that is ultimately fair.

By my own personal definition, influence is all that—but it should also have both party's best interests in mind.

Power, on the other hand, is the ability to get someone to do something that they might not normally do, or to coerce or directly force a person into a certain action or state of mind regardless of who it can benefit. Therefore, the power to influence is a significant one. Lord Acton stated, "All power tends to corrupt, and absolute power corrupts absolutely."

We've all seen the destructive results of a "bad influence" on our children, our friends, and our leaders. Therefore, I regard the concept of influence as a most precious responsibility. So, the subtlety lies in the careful use of both influence and power, because they do go together. If you can influence someone, you indeed have power, and I like to look at influence as offshoots of inspiration and motivation.

Leadership normally goes hand in hand with power, and I have held many positions of leadership. Whether it was during my 26-year career as a naval officer and diplomat, six years as an executive in industry, as an adjunct professor, or as executive director of the Pima County Democratic Party in Tucson, Arizona, I have also needed to consciously discern when I am using power versus when I am using influence. As Ben Parker told his nephew Peter in the Spider-Man movie, "with great power comes great responsibility."

Knowing the difference and applying it to how we interact with others will determine the amount of influence we have, how it is received, and, ultimately, how it will define the tone of your organization.

I teach a section on power in my political science course at Pima Community College in Tucson. I know that those in leadership, by default, are placed in a position of power and thereby bestowed with automatic influence. The Machiavellian school of leadership states that it is better to be feared than loved and that the point is to acquire power and then do everything necessary to keep it. The key word here is "fear." Influence can be wielded through fear. The threat of the removal of one's head in Machiavelli's Italian Renaissance days definitely influenced folks to obey. However, to quote the Greeks (in particular, Socrates' writings on Plato), knowledge leads to happiness. Plato draws the connection that it is not fear but knowledge that will influence the masses to do the right thing because all humans seek the notion of happiness above all else. Eventually, fear will oftentimes be challenged with rebellion. Therefore, Plato stated that by offering knowledge, human beings would naturally be inspired to follow the most virtuous path. So, we have a choice: "Do it or else" or "do it because." Both choices require influence and inspiration, but one does not require violence.

So, where does leadership fit in? Whether it's in the military, industry, or the athletic field, those being led are looking for direction, guidance, motivation, inspiration, and quite frankly, a reason to believe in their leader and the mission. In the military, I always had enough time to convey the reasons why what we were doing was important, necessary, or simply the right thing to do. There is a subtle difference between power and influence when the recipient believes they actually have a choice, and more importantly, a stake in decisions.

In the military, we were trained for the possibility of combat. In times of war or potential conflict, it becomes necessary to lead troops without the luxury of discussion and debate. Orders are issued, and they are followed. In the throes of crisis management, the only influence you may have should have been ingrained long before the crisis happens. This is where responsibility and accountability are entrusted in the leaders that we groom. Therefore, peacetime leadership does have the luxury of taking the time to gain the trust of those being led.

I've learned three essential lessons about influencers. First, we have a responsibility to others. Therefore, we have to always check ourselves and be sure that our intentions are altruistic and will serve the person well, not the other way around. If you put your own interests first, the individual you're influencing may actually choose to go in a direction that could be harmful to them or others. In a volunteer organization, some may think it is much easier to get things done when we are working towards a common goal—and not being paid. But this is where being influential is important because nothing will get accomplished otherwise, and the bigger the team, the harder it is to get things done. When I was in charge of fundraising for a non-profit organization, I led a team of five people. They looked to me for leadership, took my requests at face value, and we made historic amounts that year. The following year, I expanded the team and found it much harder to influence them because more influencers were involved. This is where it gets tricky and we have to yield our influential power to the greater good. I made the decision to step back and let others decide the outcome rather than force my own decision. But in this example, the decisions were merely aesthetic. They were not life threatening, so we must measure the worth of the outcome when pushing for our own influence. In a time crunch, when a split-second decision must be made to save lives and we are convinced our decision is the right action, we must have the confidence to influence others to do the right thing. If the outcome is not life or death, it's best to use discernment and choose our battles wisely.

Second, we need to keep the big picture in mind. Is what or who we are trying to influence a mere steppingstone to our ultimate goal, mission, or vision? For example, trying to influence a larger strategic end by chipping away at lower level goals could end up fatiguing others who will not stay the course for the big finish. On the other hand, sometimes you may need to take care of short-term goals to ensure that the big picture will unfold or become clear as time goes on. In Madagascar, I had to accompany their president and his entourage on a diplomatic visit to the United States. When we landed at a stopover in Atlanta, we got word that then-U.S. Secretary of State Condoleeza Rice had to cancel her portion of our visit due to another national security incident. The Malagasy president was furious. He was a very egotistical man and wanted to board the plane and return to Madagascar. I knew that if he canceled, it would not bode well for relations between our nations. At the time, we needed Madagascar to help with counter piracy efforts against Al Qaeda in the Mozambique Channel. Madagascar, a third world country, needed support from the U.S. in everything from humanitarian assistance to military and economic partnerships. It took me the entire two hour layover to use my influence to convince him to keep our schedule and meet with many of the other State Department and White House officials who were on the agenda. I had no power over him, but I had built a relationship with him through past meetings and conversations to where he trusted me.

Third, right makes might. This principle comes from my personal musical theater influence. In the musical Camelot, Merlin convinces King Arthur that the opposite adage, might makes right, was responsible for all the ills in the world, and hence, the age of chivalry was truly called on the carpet. I have learned, through observation in the military, that when the United States attempted to coerce another country through sheer military power or threat of economic sanctions, it may have worked in the short term, but we ended up making more enemies. When, however, we first attempted and succeeded in diplomatic measures at influencing countries to join the fight against issues such as terrorism, human or drug trafficking, or the proliferation of weapons, the use of power became unnecessary. The moral high ground nearly always influenced individuals in other countries to do the right thing. I was personally involved in a groundbreaking strategy during the global war on terror. "The Indirect Approach" was created by the Commander of Special Operations Command Pacific (SOCOM), U.S. Army General David Fridovich, for whom I worked in the Asian-Pacific theater of operations. We successfully eradicated Al Qaeda from several islands in the Philippines merely by supporting and building up the local civilian population while giving full credit to the local government. We did not sweep in with guns blazing. We ignored the enemy and built an infrastructure, creating peace, jobs, and a viable economy. We influenced a country not to side with terrorists without using force, but pure diplomatic and support influence, and achieved greater results than we would have with fear and might. Right makes might.

When I look at what has influenced me, reading books, going to plays and concerts, and watching movies and documentaries have all impacted me one way or another. Our first influencers and role models, of course, are our caregivers. In fact, those who affect our lives from birth through age five are crucial to the fundamental development of who we are and who we become as human beings and as influencers to others.

As the eldest of three girls, I spent a lot of time alone with my mother, Hiroko, whose influence has guided me to this day. Her influences were based on character, ethics, knowing right from wrong, and as a Japanese immigrant, there were a lot of cultural influences built in as well. The notions of politeness, humility, hard work, and teamwork fundamentally defined who she was, as well as the notion in her Japanese culture of beauty for beauty's sake and learning for learning's sake, not just for an end goal. My father, Bill, a product of the Great Depression and World War II, was influenced in a different way. He spent his entire life defending the underdog. He felt it was his duty to stand up to bullies and champion those without power. He was generous with his modest income and splurged on his daughters or gave most of his money away. That was a direct influence of the Great Depression. Rather than "save for a rainy day," his motto was, "don't let that dollar bill burn a hole in your pocket." Both of my parents influenced me, for better or for worse.

We've all seen the colorful, gummy bracelets with the initials WWJD (What Would Jesus Do?). Sometimes such simple reminders serve as the strongest influencers because they keep our moral compass focused. In a heated discussion or altercation, the decision to not throw a punch (verbal or otherwise) sometimes requires taking a breath and recalling who would disapprove. These lasting influencers can be parents, children, teachers, friends, philosophers, spiritual leaders, or characters—anyone whose opinion you value. I could order so many of the same bracelets with different initials: What would my mom do? What would Mr. Nimmo do? What would Candace do? What would Alex do? What would Ricky do? What would Scottie do? They are my angels who constantly keep me on course.

As influencers, we must be attentive to shift our leadership style depending on who we are leading and what type of organization or project we are overseeing. I discovered that leading sailors as a naval officer during wartime overseas was very different from overseeing volunteers and fundraisers as a nonprofit executive director in a local community. You must be flexible and adaptable, and you must know your audience—I mean really, truly know them and what makes them tick. Their background and total culmination of their life experiences, good, bad, and ugly, will determine how much they are willing or open to being influenced by you. You simply can't use the same influential style on every person.

In my first job as a Navy Ensign, I was assigned as a watch officer, hunting Soviet submarines in the Pacific Ocean. My team had very young sailors, both men and women, during the height of the Cold War. Detection of a submarine had to be reported instantly so that U.S. aircraft, submarines, and ships could be notified of their locations. There were times I had to be stern in my commands to get the sailors to pay attention and not goof off. They were between 18-28 years old. I was only 22, younger than half of them. On my very first watch, one of my senior sailors showed up pretty late to the midnight shift. Smoking was still allowed back then, and the sailor, cigarette in hand, walked into the room with a very loud and cocky attitude and rolled his eyes at me. He had never had a female officer in charge. He then flicked his cigarette into a trash can and caused a fire. My leadership style as a small woman was always couched with kind yet firm authority. I never yelled or really showed anger in front of my troops. But with a blazing fire, I had to yell across the room for them to get extinguishers and remove mounds of surrounding classified documents from potential destruction. It was put out instantly, and the sailor was pretty humbled. I continued to yell at him, something I'm not proud of today, but we shook it off in minutes and went back to work. Weeks later, after I got to know my troops better, another sailor showed up late. He was only 18, extremely shy, was bullied in the barracks, and had grown up with a terrible home life. He spilled an entire mug of coffee on an electronic communications console. I made the decision to bite my tongue, walk over, look him in the eye, and kindly ask him to clean it up and (for the millionth time) remind him to please not to have liquids near electronics. Had I shown visible or audible anger, it would have only served to beat down an already beaten sailor. Both sailors went on to work doubly hard to gain my respect. We kept in touch, and they both wrote me letters years later to thank me for influencing their decision to stay in the Navy.

The top characteristics of great influencers are honesty, genuine concern, communication skills, and past success that fosters credibility. Great influencers also hone their ability to impact others through practice and failure. You are not going to learn until you fail.

While I believe the capacity to influence is both innate and taught, for the most part, influential leaders are made by experience. Some influencers may have an inborn charming personality that causes folks to follow them into the fire. Others may have learned how to impart just the right words at the right time to motivate others. Then there are those who influence by example and sheer presence because they have gone through enough things in life to know how to lead. Use of a good sense of humor and a quick wit also doesn't hurt! My ability to influence was born from confidence in my training and in my education. After that, though, I had to immediately gain the trust of those under me through honest, direct, and frequent communication to be best positioned to influence them—and keep in mind that the best communicators are those who know how to listen first. Otherwise, it is not communicating, but rather, dictating. In short, the greatest gift we can give to those who follow us is to live, learn, and pass on knowledge.

My reward as an influencer has been seeing others achieve happiness as they meet their goals and feel good about themselves. They, in turn, go on to make the world a better place. My goal as an influencer is to strive to bring out the very best in others. After my many years of learning, failing, and succeeding, I have an obligation to help guide (or influence) others to make good decisions that will lead to success and happiness. I've learned that teaching, or *altruistic influencing,* is not a zero sum game. By passing on knowledge, our success and happiness spreads exponentially. I plan to pass on my knowledge through books, speaking engagements, and ongoing leadership in nonprofit and teaching arenas in an effort to positively influence others—at least in my little corner of the world.

I challenge you to live, learn, and inspire others. Inspiration is influence. Use it wisely and generously.

Catherine Ripley has lived and worked in over 80 countries around the world, speaks three languages, and is a professional musician, teacher, and mother. Her unique background in leadership began as one of the first women to attend the U.S. Naval Academy and spans a 26-year career as a naval officer and diplomat, six years in industry, as executive director of the Pima County Democratic Party in Arizona, and continues as an adjunct professor of political science in Tucson, Arizona. Contact Catherine at cathyripley@yahoo.com

9

Beyond My Imaginings

Patrice Schaffer

INFLUENCE STARTS AND ends with relationships—and relationships are strengthened by how much you and the other person influence each other and help one another.

My husband, Mike, and I have been married over 33 years. He is very even keeled, very slow to anger, and loves to volunteer and help people. It is his very nature to do so, and that has had a huge influence on me and on our children. One thing he and I often laugh about is how, instead of using the word "volunteered," we use "voluntold." Both of us are pretty involved in church and similar groups. Someone will say, "We need x, y, z," and he will say, "My wife can help you with that," or I will say, "My husband can help you with that." We go back and forth telling each other, "Hey, I just voluntold you!" It's rubbed off on our kids as well. My youngest daughter is a musical theater major, and she'll often come and say, "Dad, I need you to go here at this time because they need help on the set, and I told them you would do it." He got voluntold!

It's a great way to have influence—as I have learned over a varied career path that saw me work for about 12 years in various programmer analyst jobs before leaving the corporate world in 2000 to stay at home with my children. Being a stay-at-home mommy didn't work out as well with me because I am such an extrovert. A few months after being home, I joined a YMCA program as an aide before and after school. It was the perfect job because my girls could come with me to work. In 2005, Mike was working on a construction project building a Christian-based preschool called the Mustard Seed. He told the director that I was home with the children, had worked at the YMCA, and that I was looking to return to work to do something with kids. I was employed at the childcare center doing whatever I could do as an aide, like setting up lunches, cleaning the bathrooms, changing diapers, you name it. I was grateful to be able to converse with other adults while having my children with me at the same time. Having a background in business management and computer science, I found myself evaluating systems and processes and eventually transitioned into the role as the assistant director. In 2014, I realized I wanted to go back into the technology field and found my current job with navitend (the company's branding has all lower-case lettering), a Managed Service Provider (MSP) that provides leadership and technology services to businesses and non-profits in New Jersey, New York, and Philadelphia, Pennsylvania.

At the center, I found that I could sit and pray with parents when they came in, as well as pray with kids when they were having issues. It gave me an influence I'd never had previously in my career, and as a lifelong Catholic, I loved being able to blend my spiritual life with my professional one. One of my personal sayings is, "If we trust God and follow Him, He will bless us beyond our imaginings." I certainly found that to be the case at the Mustard Seed, where my good friend, Carol, who was director at the Mustard Seed, became such an influence on me by showing me how we can teach young children and influence them to pray as well. One of my most precious moments at the center was when a four-year-old boy stood up during circle time, asked if everyone would join him in prayer, and then led a prayer with all the teachers and children. What really stood out for me was that it doesn't matter who you are, where you are, or how old you are. You can still pray aloud and lead others in prayer to God. It was something that will be with me forever.

Personally, I believe I've had a big influence on my children. I have three girls. My oldest, Heather, is 29 and a mom, so I have a grandson. I also have 25-year-old, Katey, and 20-year-old, Maggie. The influence comes in how they see my husband and I handle things. How you react during times of critical need, uncertainty, and fearfulness is so important. It's not that you won't have those thoughts yourself as a spouse, parent, or coworker, but it's through what you do to make those situations better that your influence blooms. Mike and I have discovered that we are not only able to influence them during hard times, but they influence us in a good way through their reactions. We raised them to pray and set a good example, always relying on God and faith.

In terms of who else has influenced me, Mr. Parslow was a good friend of the family who basically took on a father figure role for my brother and I when we were younger. Mr. Parslow later became a huge influence on my husband and kids until he passed away about seven years ago. He told it like it was, but he really cared about us, our future, and about what we were doing in our lives and whether it was the right thing to be doing. He wasn't shy about telling us if we made a bad choice. Mr. Parslow taught me an influencer can be any person in your life who really gives you meaning—where you can look back 20, 30, 40 years later and remember that person, that time, and what they did for you.

I discovered another valuable lesson in influence when a friend from one of my corporate jobs asked me to consider selling Mary Kay cosmetics with her and invited me to join her at a Mary Kay convention. My friend was a reserved, very corporate sort of person who I could not imagine wanting to go out and sell cosmetics by having parties at people's houses. When we got to the convention, I quickly discovered how inspiring (and loud) the events can be. There we were, the two of us among hundreds of other ladies, and everyone was standing up, clapping their hands, and singing this outrageous song, "I've got the Mary Kay spirit down in my heart—where?" At first, I thought, *Wow! We are so out of place*, but you know the saying, "If you can't beat 'em, join 'em!" I stood up, started to chant and clap, and my friend was mortified. I ended up selling Mary Kay products for nine years, and I was so successful I once went on stage in Dallas, Texas in the "Queens Court of Sales" and actually got to meet Mary Kay in person. It was truly a "God given" experience. She said, "If you act enthusiastic, you will become enthusiastic." I've found that to be so true. Enthusiasm is contagious, and when others lack enthusiasm, I've been able to have an encouraging influence on them. As I see what God has placed in my heart and in my life, I know I've got a lot to be enthusiastic about. During my time with Mary Kay, I also learned that when we put God first in our lives, we don't have to worry about much else, and that our families should come next, followed by our career.

I've also been blessed beyond my imaginings as an influencer in my current job at navitend. When I first joined the company, I handled the daily accounting responsibilities, adding inside sales support and assisting in quoting and procurement a few months later. When I was eventually asked to become part of a leadership team put together by the CEO, I enthusiastically agreed, eventually taking on more of a business development role by branding and marketing the company. Small businesses are always challenged to get all of their work done, and I've learned that a business succeeds whenever the staff deals with tasks and challenges proactively. But even more important is the power of prayer in the workplace. At navitend, prayer offers us peace and an eternal perspective that comes from acknowledging God as being real and present. I take great joy in knowing that a meeting at navitend will start and end in prayer and that any requests I have can be prayed about in the office.

I have a passion in my marketing role at navitend, and it is my goal to be a good influencer at work to help the company move forward and succeed. It is important for me to let others outside of work know what I do for navitend because I am a representative of the company regardless of where I am and who I am with at that moment. I've also made sure that I have my own personal support group outside of work made up of other women in business. These women are going through many of the same things in all different business spaces. At navitend, I've discovered that I can be the voice of all the other great women around me (I'm the only full-time female staff member at the company), and I want to influence other women, especially younger ones who want to pursue a career in technology. I currently serve in a few different "women in business" groups, and three years ago started an annual panel discussion of women called "Share Your Success." It's a truly great event where women share their personal journeys to success, the challenges they have faced, and their most important life lessons.

The benefits I've experienced from an influencer in a work-related job started right out of college. I was a computer science major, but coming out of college, I didn't want to be a programmer at first, so I ended up working in the accounting field. It was 1987, and computers were just becoming popular and being added to offices as a "tool" to help make everyone more productive. Microsoft had just released Windows 2.0, and I was able to use the very first version of Excel. It was an exciting time, and all the knowledge I gained helped me in my future. Once I felt more confident, I realized information technology was where I was heading. I changed jobs and became a backup administrator where I ran computer data backups for a company that provided AT&T gift certificates based on long distance usage. I worked 8:00 p.m. to 8:00 a.m., alternating between three- and four-day work weeks. Newly married then with no children, it was a decent job and the pay was really great, allowing us to build our first home, but was I bored. So, I picked up some programming manuals, read a lot, and my manager asked me to stay an extra hour every day to work side by side with another programmer. I became a programmer analyst for that company within six months. My manager influenced me by seeing my potential, intervening, and moving me forward.

Through my work and my personal responsibilities, as my husband and I began raising a family, influence was given and received through the relationships I built and established. Keeping those relationships healthy is a reward in and of itself. It creates camaraderie and fosters respect. I used to be a district commissioner of the New Jersey Youth Soccer Organization. Basically, I kept track of groups of children playing soccer on traveling teams. Many years later, I was organizing an event for our church, and I went to the municipal building downtown to get some permits. As I gave a woman my application, I thought she looked familiar.

She turned to me and said, "I think I know you." She thought about it another moment, then told me, "Now I remember. You helped my eight-year-old son in soccer. He was crying so much because he didn't know how to sign his card." She was referring to an identification card required for him to compete in the games. She continued, "He didn't know how to sign it in cursive. You said to him, 'Listen, just take the pen and make any mark you can make on the card, and that will be your signature.' I always remembered that about you and how nice you were to him." Later on, even that very brief relationship was still there.

From that, I was reminded that we don't want to sever a relationship just because we might be in a different environment now than we were in the past. We should never forget those people, whether we influence them, or they influence us. About six years ago, my husband "voluntold" me to help with an organization called Operation Chillout (OCO), New Jersey's oldest all-volunteer mobile outreach for homeless veterans. I have worked with them on their annual fundraiser called Vets Summer Fest, and the relationships I have made have had a huge influence on me. OCO owes its existence to the men and women of the United States Armed Forces for providing the freedoms we hold dear. OCO was founded in 2000 to help a group of homeless veterans living in the open under a railroad trestle in northern New Jersey, and it provides emergency supplies and survival gear to the most vulnerable members of our communities regardless of their religious affiliation, ethnic heritage, or state of life.

The first year I helped, I realized that the grounds at the event could host at least 100 or more vendors, but only 12 vendors were in attendance that day. The event was able to raise some money but not a substantial amount with the time and effort from all the volunteers. I realized people knew little about OCO and what they did. We had no donor list and a small profile. It was quite the challenge, but I went to work, and the job quickly educated me about needing to grow the charity's brand while establishing my own credibility as someone who could speak with a clear voice about the organization. I broadened my influence by speaking to funders and to the public regarding the issues OCO cared about in serving homeless veterans. It wasn't an easy road, but I had the help of many individuals and organizations such as the Knights of Columbus, the Columbiettes (women members of the auxiliary affiliated with the Knights of Columbus Council), and many local churches. Within five years, we had over 100 vendors and over 3,000 people in attendance at the annual fundraiser. The best part was that we were able to triple our fundraising efforts for the organization.

As a fundraiser, I had to think so carefully about influence. One thing I learned to help increase my influence as a fundraiser was my likability. I had to show a real interest in what I was doing and the charity I was representing, and I had to be authentic by showing how much I was in tune with the vision of helping homeless veterans. Lastly, my personal brand had to be strong enough in relation to making a difference in the lives of homeless veterans. I extended my individual profile so that when people looked me up online or via social media, they saw me as the person of influence for the cause. It was a remarkable experience.

When I consider my future as an influencer, I have come to understand that what I do is enough. I'm a work in progress and becoming better at recognizing when I am overworking or committing myself to too many responsibilities at any given time. In addition, I've learned that I shouldn't allow myself to get so worked up about letting people down or thinking that I wasn't able to produce something good enough to contain real value. I've been down the road before where I have disliked the person I see in the mirror because I was constantly not meeting the higher standards that I set for myself. If that's you, turn those thoughts off! As an influencer, the greatest takeaway you can get out of reading this book is to know and say to yourself: "I am doing what I can do. There is effort. That is good." It may not be perfect, but only *God* is perfect!

Your best is more than enough as long as you continue to prioritize relationships—and remember how much God has blessed you beyond your imaginings.

Three things are most important to **Patrice Schaffer**: her faith, her family, and helping others. Her current position is working as a marketing and business development strategist at navitend, an information technology company located in Stanhope, New Jersey. Patrice spends a large amount of time volunteering for many different organizations and causes. Her education background includes a bachelor's degree in computer information systems with a concentration in business management from York College of Pennsylvania. She loves to connect with people on LinkedIn or contact her at pschaffer@navitend.com

10

The Outcomes of Influence

Sharon Wamble-King

IT WAS JUST a speech, no different from any of the others I'd given before about me and my journey as a professional.

But that's the thing about influence. You just never know when something you say or do is going to make a huge difference in someone's life.

The young lady came up to me afterward, a timid smile on her face. "That was so inspiring," she said. "You really made me feel so proud to be an African American woman."

But then she began talking about how she really wanted to do certain things in her life, but felt that she couldn't, in part because she didn't have a college degree. Even worse, she started speaking about herself in a very negative way.

"Wait a minute," I told her. "Let's go talk."

Right there and then, I stopped everything and invited her up to my office in the executive suite. She hesitated. "I'm not allowed to go up there."

"Well," I said, taking her hand, "now you will."

I guided her into the elevator. "Oh, if my boss' boss sees me up here," she nervously said, "I'm gonna get in trouble."

"Don't worry about that," I said as the elevator began heading upward. "If you get in trouble, call me."

I led her into my office, closed the door, and cancelled my next appointments. We ended up talking for about an hour. I started with her self-esteem and her view of herself because of her lack of a degree. I spoke to her about the God-given gifts she had and that she was at the company for a reason. "You are a woman who has a lot of potential, a lot to contribute, and a lot of value." It wasn't a matter of pumping her up. It was all about helping her recognize the treasure that was in her life and how she needed to share her life with people. I also explained to her how her negative self-talk was forming barriers that would hold her back. I concluded, "Love all of the things you are and look at yourself differently."

About a year later, she told me, "After talking to you, I went and applied for a job that I never thought I would be qualified for. I was scared, but I got the position. You changed my life forever because of the encouragement you gave me that day and the way you started me thinking about who I am."

You just can't get that kind of influence from reading a book or taking a training class. You get it from leading with your heart. I had discernment about how that young lady could be so much more than she believed herself to be—and now she is!

That's influence. Influence is the ability to motivate, inspire, compel, shift beliefs and attitudes, and reframe paradigms to produce an outcome that changes the way people see the world and interact with others. My influence with that young woman began with the discernment I had about her that created within her the self-awareness to enhance, build upon, and have clarity about who she was. I wanted her to see herself differently. Self-awareness is the scaffolding of the heart that will allow her to stand on those experiences and grow as a person.

Influence is also asserted when we are a role model, open doors for others that haven't been opened before, and behave in positive ways by being courageous, vulnerable, and trustworthy. These are pathways to influence as others are magnetized to the essence of our power, our passion, and our purpose. When I studied to become a John Maxwell certified teacher, speaker, and coach, John facilitated a lesson during which he focused on words that start with "in" like "inspire," "insight," and "innovate." If we look at the source of those actions, he said, it is coming from the inside. It's about our positionality, where we ask ourselves, "How am I standing? Who is the wellspring of my thoughts and beliefs, and how are they manifested in my actions? Am I positioned in a place of rejection, self-pity, discouragement, and doubt, or am I standing in gratefulness, enlightenment, confidence, and connection?" Oftentimes, just the energy of our positionality will attract and inspire others to think about our example, follow us, and consider for themselves, "How did they do it? Maybe I can do it, too!"

There are times when we influence others without being in a position of authority, shaping another person's attitudes, behaviors, thoughts, and beliefs without explicitly being given the permission to do so. Sometimes, I've even had people say to me, "You are a risk taker. I could never do what you are doing." Even though I am not influencing them to actually do what they see me do or say what I am saying, I am a catalyst for them to look at their lives, consider other choices, and imagine new possibilities. It is like what the Apostle Paul said in the Bible in 1 Corinthians 1 when he encouraged others to follow him as he followed Christ. As we live our lives the right way, others will want to emulate us.

Years ago, I hired a young lady who had just graduated from college. I had hundreds of resumes for the position, and everyone told me not to hire her. They wanted me to choose someone more experienced. Yet I saw something in the young lady, and I hired her. I did everything I could to help her build a pathway for her career in corporate communications. I was a mentor and a coach. I spent extra time with her in the evenings. I wanted to be the right kind of professional for her to see how to build relationships, and I made sure she met the right kind of people to do so. As she watched and learned from me, she could actually see how I was building relationships, performing, being creative and innovative, and dealing with conflict. She was like a sponge—and today she is the vice president of internal communication for an international financial brokerage company. I am so proud of her. She always says that I gave her the foundation she needed to excel, and it was my joy to do so.

At the top of the list of my greatest influencers are my parents. My mother, Thula, and father, Dorn, moved from Arkansas to California during World War II to work in the Bay Area shipping yards. They had dreams and visions of a better life. They worked hard. My father worked three jobs to support his family. My mother also worked. Both of them ended up going back to school. They wanted to make sure their children had a better life.

Therefore, I grew up in the radical Bay Area of the 1960's. My parents influenced me and my brother, Marvin, to be visionaries, risk takers, and activists who looked for ways we could help others. They often did this in very practical ways. We were not on welfare, but we were not rich. At the beginning of every month, when my father got his paycheck, we would have a family meeting, write down all the bills, and pray for wisdom and direction. There was never enough money, yet the first thing on the list of items to be paid were the tithes to our church—and the decision-making process was influenced by obedience to Scripture. Then, we would decide what bills we would pay that month. They reminded us that they were sacrificing and working to make sure we got an education—that we, as African Americans, got the same education others did.

Berkeley, California was segregated then. As a kid, I took part in civil rights marches and demonstrations for fair housing and equal rights. My parents were big believers in integrated schools because their experiences in the south showed them that segregated schools did not provide the quality of education they should've. Therefore, we moved to a different neighborhood so my brother and I could have an opportunity to go to an integrated school. I finally did just that for the first time in sixth grade, and I made the honor roll. The next year, though, I had to return to a segregated school while my father and many other parents led a fight to allow black students to attend the all-white school in the El Cerrito hills. They prevailed, and I was among the first 100 black kids from the segregated school to go to the all-white one.

That's the outcome of influence.

Another person who influenced me was Bishop Elmer Elijah (E.E.) Cleveland, pastor of Ephesians Church of God in Christ in Berkeley. I always thought he was an extremely caring man. This was a man who was called on by churches all over the world to preach and teach, yet no matter where I saw him, he would hug me and make me think I was the only person in the world and that I was so highly valued. He would pray for me. I always knew that when he prayed for me, I was "prayed for."

The church I grew up in was one of the largest churches in Berkeley at the time. People flocked there from all over the world to hear Bishop E.E. Cleveland preach. When I was at the University of the Pacific, I was a disc jockey with a gospel program, and I was trying to figure out how to get an audience. I asked him if he would come down to my school and preach on my program. He was always traveling, but it was Founder's Day at the school, and there were going to be thousands of people on campus. He was scheduled to get on a plane to go do a series of revivals, but he cancelled his trip and a member of the church drove him and my mother down to my school. The studio was set up for me for the day, and the recording could be heard on the loudspeaker on the street.

This was a predominately white school. There were probably fewer than a hundred black people in the entire student body. When Bishop E.E. Cleveland arrived, all these young white kids started looking at him—and he just started hugging on them. The kids hadn't seen ministers that didn't have collars like a priest, and they certainly hadn't met too many black preachers. Then he walked into the studio, and he knew what to do. The "on air" light came on, and he said, "I'm here to preach the gospel." Before you knew it, the whole studio was full of students and staff. I went outside, and there were people lined up everywhere. He preached five sermons, and folks were giving him standing ovations. Arriving in the pulpit the next day, everybody was surprised to see him because he was supposed to be on an evangelistic trip. He said, "I want you to know I spent all day at the university yesterday with Sis Wamble's daughter preaching the gospel on the school's radio station." He was so happy, and he did all of that out of his love for me and others. I saw someone who was world famous humble himself and spend a day with college students so he could change their lives. In the process, he forever impacted mine. He was so humbly intimate with us that we lovingly called him "Dad" Cleveland.

If you really want to leave a legacy and pour into people, it is not about you. It is about them. God put us here as His hands and His feet, His eyes and His ears, to impact the lives of other people. Is being God's paintbrush on the canvas of someone else's life an outcome of influence? It certainly is.

As a professional, I am a people strategist who supports leaders at all levels so they can align with their purpose and passion and act with insight and intention to be the best they can be, all while ensuring that those in their sphere of influence reach the pinnacle of success and significance. Success is adding value to myself, which is laudable, but significance is adding value to others. I focus on co-creating a space for people to soar to the zenith of their potential through communication, engagement, and influence.

I've had quite a journey, and many influencers have propelled me all along the way. After graduate school, I worked a variety of different jobs before landing at Kaiser Permanente. That was followed by service at William M. Mercer, Arthur Andersen, LLP, Aetna, Inc., and with one of the largest health insurers based in Florida—with the launch (and relaunch) of my own company, The WambleKing Group, in the midst of it all. It's been an amazing ride, and one of my most significant influencers was a mentor, Les Walker, who took me on when I first started working in corporate America. I didn't have a clue what corporate America was about, but he saw my potential. He told me, "Sharon, you are as green as the lawn outside. I am going to help you." He said we would have a mentoring relationship, but no one would know, adding, "We will meet once a week." He taught me everything from how to go to executive dinners to how to behave at the workplace, what kinds of things to talk about to excel, and what to expect so I could anticipate and plan my professional development. Another influencer in my career was the vice president of communications at Kaiser Permanente, Robert Hughes. He remains one of the smartest men I know, and he is an introvert. Yet people just sat at his feet and wanted to partake of his wisdom. He was kind, generous, and gracious. His sense of humor and the way he would think through issues impacted how I saw myself and acted as a communications professional.

That's another outcome of influence.

Finally, there were those in the community at large who were influential by helping me see the world in a very different way and said they saw something in me that I didn't see in myself. I was very quiet in school. In a history class at the University of the Pacific, I never said a word. When I got my history paper back from the professor, I had an F. I had never gotten an F in my life. I was distraught. I later went to see the professor in his office, and I was crying. I asked him what I did wrong.

He smiled. "It's nice to hear your voice, Sharon," he said calmly. "I know that you know more than anybody else in that class, but I can't get you to say anything. I figured if I gave you an F, you'd at least say something to me."

Then he told me to look in his grade book. I had an A. He gave me the alleged F just to get me to talk.

That's an outcome of influence delivered in a compelling way.

As an influencer, I have learned there is a difference between coaching and mentoring. Mentoring is sharing from my own experiences to shape the way people see themselves and their situations. It is empathetic influence that says, "I've been there before. Let me tell you what I did." That can be limiting, though, because the fact that I've experienced something doesn't mean they are going to experience it in the same way. It may give them inspiration and insight, but in many ways, when I am a mentor, I am imposing my worldview on them. Therefore, I am much more of a coach as an influencer. The coach recognizes the intrinsic value of the individual and approaches them with the notion that they are a treasure. They are full of value, and my job is to help them recognize themselves and to unearth what is there—like I did with the young woman who heard me speak. I help them put together the pieces they already have. It is empowering because I'm asking the questions, providing the prompts, and allowing the silence in the conversation so they can process it all for themselves. To see how people blossom when you have them doing work on themselves, rather than you telling them what to do, is incredible. They own the solution. They own the position. They own the viewpoint.

I once worked with a young man who was supervised by another colleague who worked for me. He needed guidance on a big project, and I was so careful about imposing myself on him. I was older than him, and I had a lot more experience. I didn't want to push him into wearing the straitjacket that is "me." I wanted him to be his own blossoming, fabulous, valuable self. I knew he had to learn within that context. We worked together, and I asked him a few questions. Then I instructed him to come back to me with what he thought we should do. I gave him some guidelines, thoughts, and resources. He later told my boss, "Sharon does to me what my baseball coach does to me. I am competitive by nature. My coach would never give me the answer. He always said I had the answer and then gave me a couple of guidelines and things to think about. He said I knew what the answer was and how to get it done, and he trusted me to do it. I would therefore push myself based on his coaching of me to get there. Sharon does the same thing to me."

I had no idea I was influencing him in that way—but I was thrilled to hear it. That's one of the several rewards to being an influencer. You'll be able to uplift someone to be the best they can be. You'll feel like you've been able to make a positive contribution in the world. You'll be an instrument in God's hands to assist in their progress towards their dreams and their vision of themselves in their highest potential. It's not about ego. It's about watching others flourish. That's really fulfilling.

As far as what I see myself doing to continue to be an influencer in the years to come, I have to start with self-awareness—being what God wants me to be and doing what he wants me to do with those who he wants me to do it. I need to be in humble obedience to Him in order to enable them to love themselves, believe in themselves, and trust in God. As I pursue my doctorate, I've always wanted to write, consult, teach, and speak. I'm praying I will be positioned to do those things in the next chapter He has in store for me.

In the end, I want to use the uniqueness that I have to inspire others in their uniqueness. I am giving you the seed. You are the one growing the garden.

And, yes, that's the outcome of influence.

Sharon Wamble-King is a lifelong learner, passionate communication strategist, organizational change leader, consultant, and coach. She is pursuing a doctorate in leadership and change from Antioch University, and she possesses decades of experience in corporate, consulting, ecumenical, and not-for-profit environments. She helps people and organizations learn, grow, and transform to leverage their opportunities to reimagine and reinvent purpose-driven futures. Contact Sharon at sharon@thewamblekinggroup.com

11

A Place at the Table

Dr. Karockas Watkins

"**THIS IS WHAT** I want to do, and here is why I want to do it."

Being an influencer starts with looking for opportunities, thinking about those opportunities, having the discernment to know what opportunities are best—and then being willing to speak up, step in, and step out to place yourself in that situation, and get a place at the table.

That's what I've done throughout my career—and it's what I continue to do as a leadership mentor to several domestic and international leaders, and in my work as CEO/ president of Vision Excellence Company, my leadership and business consulting firm.

An influencer is someone who has the ability to change the character and behavior within a person or an organization. As you find your gifts and your talent, you then see how you can work those abilities within a system or a group of people to get them across. The worst thing in the world is to have a gift or talent that you can't use. That's why you have to figure out how you can use them for the greater good outside of your circle of influence to help the community and beyond.

That comes through discovery by building relationships. An influencer is constantly building new and better relationships. This goes beyond basic networking, and it does not happen overnight. For example, with Joe Newberry, chief executive officer of Redstone Federal Credit Union, I found a mentor and sponsor who was already an influencer and who would listen to me. I expressed what I wanted to get done and why. "I have people skills," I told him. "I have a background with people and in engineering. I think I can make a difference. I am the CEO of a company that influences people in the city, so I want to use what I have to help." Then I poured out my heart and demonstrated what I had to offer.

I was not automatically put in a position of influence, but I was asked to talk to a few people, attend a few functions, tell my story, and observe what was going on. Over time, as I built that relationship and others, I got to the table. Now, I'm able to influence the influencers, people of power I otherwise may not have had access to, as well as those I lead to hear and follow some of the philosophies that I live by. In summer 2020, for example, I was able to influence a financial wealth company to start a new internship program with the University of Alabama A&M College of Business. I also realized I had to strategically market myself in a way that was not self-serving, but for the betterment of what was going on in our community.

When I first became chief executive officer at Ability Plus Inc. in Huntsville, AL, the largest single provider in Alabama of services for people with special needs, I had an opportunity to influence leaders, teammates, and younger professionals by looking at our company's culture. In a year-and-a-half, we dramatically turned around that culture, and the company's bottom line, through teaching and mentorship. After I arrived, I saw that no one believed in what they thought they could do. In response, I first helped implement a servant leadership-style approach. This caused the staff to trust leadership with the vision that was set in front of them. I also called them to work harder and smarter for the common cause. Next, I worked with the staff to change their behavior and outlook on what was possible. I talked about going from good to great. I encouraged people to do their best and then asked the question, "Are you sure that is your best?" As a result, they went over and beyond, didn't complain, and became innovative within their own departments, doing things in a smarter and consistent way.

I've learned a variety of lessons about influence over the years. Motivational speaker and author, Les Brown, taught me to be careful of my circle, the people I hang out with, and to strive to be around people who are better than me. I learned, "If you are the smartest one in the room, you are in the wrong room." When I served on the board of a high profile company and listened to everyone around the room share their insights about how to help the organization solve problems and move forward with their strategic plans, the questions they asked and their responses to their challenges were eye opening. Their approach was at a higher level than where I was operating at the time. I listened, took notes, and since then have applied some of those same tactics to my own business initiatives.

Secondly, I've told people, "If you are going to influence, you have to learn how to influence and do it right. Look at other influencers, not famous people, and see what they do, how they respond, how they act, where they go, and what they need." An influential woman who owns a defense company invited me over to her house with a bunch of other influencers that she knew in the city. I watched her and how she introduced everyone, worked the room, and made every influencer there feel comfortable. She did it like a technician. It was my first time in that type of relaxed setting with those people, and even as we talked business, it felt more like a family reunion.

Finally, as an influencer, if you do something that may be fine in one culture but could be offensive or taken negatively in another culture, you undermine your ability to influence. Remember, influence is changing people so that they accept who you are and accept the talent, the information, and the knowledge that you bring. If you cannot do that because a person has put up a roadblock or has put their guard up against you, it doesn't make any difference how much knowledge or talent you have. You won't have an influence on them unless you know how to best engage the culture in that room

As an African American, I grew up in a culture that has its own idioms and its own way of doing things. One day, I was preparing to present my qualifications to members of a business networking organization to determine if they could use my services. A friend of mine who was white and knew my presentation style said, "Doc, you might not want to do it that way."

"What do you mean?" I asked.

"They are going to think you are bragging on yourself. You're not going to influence them to work with you because they're going to think you're making it about you."

I told him I still didn't understand. He elaborated, "They know who you are already. Just let the conversation evolve, but don't initiate it."

"I'm glad you told me that," I responded to my friend, "because in our African American culture, we let people know what we can do. Matter of fact, we give more respect to those we know are doing certain things and can talk about it."

"I understand that," he said, "but your influence won't be the same in this group if you go about it that way."

"Very good. I'll adjust, talk around it, and let it come up."

The presentation went well, they became a client—and one month later, the CEO of a contracting company who was at that presentation came to me. "I heard about the types of seminars that you do. Would you come talk to my people?" I did, and that presentation was well received.

As an influencer, seeing people and companies change is my reward. I also appreciate that others look to me for guidance. That keeps me trying to be the best I can be. Another reward is that I've met incredible people who broaden me, help me, and illustrate things that I never would have thought about without them.

The person who influenced me the most was Dr. David

Green, Jr., who was dean of the science and math department at Kettering University (formerly GMI Engineering & Management Institute) in Michigan before he retired. He chose me from a slate of students in Alabama to go to the General Motors Institute. I went there to study to be an engineer. He mentored me all five of the years I was there, and even when I wanted to quit, he challenged me to stay. He said he knew greatness was inside of me—and told me that the impossible was possible more than anyone else. Dr. Green absolutely forced me to think differently. Every time I gave him an excuse, he took the excuse off the table.

More recently, some key people in my company, particularly my chief operations officer and executive team, have exhorted me by saying, "Keep dreaming. Dream big. Don't give up. It is possible." They're not only cheerleaders, but they hold me accountable to being the best I can be, and I appreciate it. I have also benefitted greatly from the encouragement of those outside my business setting. I'm blessed with both a brother, Brandon, and brother-in-law, Marcus, who totally believe I can do anything I put my mind to. Every time I've come to a hard place where it seems I can't go any further, both of them have told me, "There's more in you. You are called to influence the world!" My wife, Audra, has fully supported me. She has believed in me, and has even told me, "I'm where I am today because of what you do, Karockas." That's even more significant considering she is the chief administrative officer in my company. It just infuses me to continue to move forward, take risks when it's time to do so, and be reminded anew of my abilities and the confidence I should have in those abilities.

To be an influencer, you need some relationship management going on so you can function outside of yourself. I'm certified to conduct seminars on emotional intelligence as it relates to business. Relationship management is the last quadrant of emotional intelligence and simply speaks to having self and social awareness: who you are, who other people are, and then putting that together to build and manage relationships.

The power to define is the power to determine destiny. If I define who I am, I know who I am—and I can then bring that into a relationship with others to find out who they are, what makes them tick, and what will compel them forward. It positions me to use who I am and who they are to better the relationship and the situation they're facing. I recall working with a man who had incredible talent to help young people, but he struggled with who he was. As I taught him about emotional intelligence, I instructed, "You need to discover your weaknesses. Find them out. Write them down. Work on your weaknesses as you identify and maximize your strengths. Then your talent can be used in a greater way, and you won't be on the defensive when someone challenges you." He ended up acquiring a new position and a major advancement.

Are people born with a natural inclination to influence others? Yes. I believe I have a gift to engage people. But that is not enough. You have to refine the gift. Influential people are taught, and you learn as you honor the influencers that have come before you, build trust with them, and then raise your engagement with them. There's a particular influencer in Alabama that is quite known in the area. He heads a multi-million dollar company. I met him at a chamber of commerce function, and I told him about myself and some of my aspirations in life. He invited me to lunch at his office—and from then on, he has become an influencer and mentor to me. He has introduced me to others with even higher levels of influence, and he's taught me much about how to maneuver in those situations.

In the future, I see myself expanding my influence in other areas, and over a more national and global scale, so I can influence others to lead in better ways and maximize the future. As you seek to become a person of influence, remember there is no table too big for you. It will take work to get to that table, learning who you are and becoming a person of value so people will let you in the door. But you cannot be afraid of making mistakes along the way because every influencer has made mistakes. Failure is part of the process of getting to the table. Then, when you get to that table, remember you're there to dine and share your very best with others.

Dr. Karockas Watkins serves as a leadership mentor to several domestic and international leaders, and he is the chief executive officer, president, and executive director of Ability Plus Inc. in Huntsville, AL. He is also CEO/ president of Vision Excellence Company, a leadership and business consulting company, board overseer of Emmanuel: The Connection Church in Madison, AL, and a business mentor and executive/leadership/life coach. Contact Karockas at karockas.watkins@ability-plus.org or karockas@vision-excellence-company.com

12

Caring on Purpose

Janelle Wood

INFLUENCE IS BEING able to model the characteristics you want others to exhibit. Therefore, if I want you to go out and walk in faith, follow your dreams, and pursue the desires of your heart, then you must see me do it first.

You must also know that I genuinely care for you.

It's my responsibility and privilege to get people to move in a direction that builds up their character and helps them find their God-given purpose and life mission. Then, great influencers are those whose determination and passion for that purpose and mission are evident. They are unrelenting. They don't back away just because an obstacle comes their way. They figure out how to get around it or how to overcome it.

Great influencers are focused. They are not distracted easily. They don't mind sitting in front and taking the hit when necessary. They are articulate, even when they stumble over their words. Finally, great influencers are kind, humble servants, and they honor those around them. They are confident but not conceited. They are not only willing to do what they ask others to do but are usually already doing it before they even request it.

I am convinced that all of us are created to be influencers. We are born with that ability; however, we need to have a teachable spirit. My first real job out of college was with a major insurance company. I was a claims adjuster who worked with policy holders, individuals involved with the policy holders' claims, attorneys, and medical providers. My supervisor recognized that I had a heart for people and that I could grasp information and run with it. One day, dressed in one of my cute pink or green dresses, I asked my supervisor what it would take for me to move into management.

"I don't want you to take this the wrong way. I think you dress really nice, but this pink and green has got to go. No one can take you seriously when you show up in a pink suit or dress." A deaconess at her church, she continued, "I need you to turn this whole wardrobe around. I need you to get corporate colors, neutrals, because right now no one takes you seriously. I can't put you on the management track at this point."

That hurt my feelings because I thought the way I dressed was cute. It also challenged my mentality, in that when I came into corporate America from college, I was a sorority girl, and it was time to start growing up. My supervisor directed me to go to a consignment shop, because I didn't make a lot of money, and put a suit on layaway each pay period, so I could gradually build up my wardrobe. She told me to get pants and skirts and shoes that were black or navy blue. I slowly changed—and as I did, I started to be placed on committees and to be taken seriously. My supervisor had a great influence on me. It was the first time someone in her position told me something that changed how I approached things. I had to be willing to allow her to speak into my life and not be offended. I respected and trusted her to tell me what she did. Those who are positioned to speak into your life are the ones you respect and trust who conduct themselves in a way that allows you to honor what they say when they speak to you.

Even now, I strive to know my audience and dress accordingly, so they'll take me seriously when I walk into a room. Dressing to have an executive presence, especially for a woman employed in a male-dominated field, is vital. As a woman, it's a shame I have to present myself a certain way in order for people to listen to me and actually realize I bring great value to the table—but some people can't get past what I look like to understand that I actually know what I am talking about.

Influencers are willing to study and learn, and they will accept rebuke, redirection, and correction when needed. They are willing to admit when they have made a mistake, recognizing that, while the mistake may be somewhat hurtful, they can submit to what needs to happen as a result of it and surrender to the process. I have learned all of these attributes of great influencers throughout my career of community service—and especially in my work as founder of the Black Mothers Forum, Inc. It is an organization dedicated to end the bloodshed in the black community, dismantle the school to prison pipeline, and restore the strength, dignity, and hope of the black community.

Through my experiences with the forum, and from my educational background in economics and biblical leadership, I've discovered that African American women make purchases to either soothe some sort of pain or to put on a front that they are doing better than they are. The clothes we wear, and even how we decide to style our hair, speak about how we see ourselves. Jesus Christ spent a lot of time working with people on their relationships with Him, with each other, and what was going on inside their hearts, and He still does today. It all comes down to what causes us to do the things we do—and our spending is directly tied to what's in our heart.

God moved me to bring forth the Black Mother's Forum because I understand that what goes on inside of the heart of a mother is going to be transferred to her child. Her habits, traditions, fears, spending habits, and how she views herself are all projected onto her children, and her children are going to project that in their lives in the way they make decisions and respond to particular situations. It's a cycle that continues. So, one of the things I believe I am called to do, because of my relationship with Jesus, is model how we as women should be responding to certain situations in our lives. Because I have surrendered my life to the Lord, He has helped me understand the things I should be focused on, and that material things are not as important as relational things. I have observed many of our young black mothers buy, buy, buy—but they don't spend enough quality time with their children, pouring, pouring, pouring into them. I encourage mothers to get an understanding of, "Why is it that we do the things we do?" Once we come to terms with the "why," then together we can influence our society for the betterment of ourselves and our children.

One of the biggest lessons I have learned in the area of influence is that what I do and how I enter into a space really matters. I have found that people watch exactly what I say and what I do. If I have a furrow on my brow, they'll make a comment about that, and it shifts their mood. I constantly have to be very responsible for my emotions and for allowing God to do whatever He is going to do through me. In my role with the Black Mothers Forum, there have been times I've had to speak in front of district school boards about racial and volatile situations that have happened to the students and their families. In these emotionally charged meetings, I'd write out my statement, and then look and dress professionally when I was called to speak. I remained calm and addressed the board passionately but respectfully. If a member of the board then responded negatively or disrespectfully to me, I remained poised and professional and completed my presentation. I'd look directly at the board member and nod to indicate that I understood what was being said, even if I didn't agree with it.

The more I modeled passion coupled with poise and professionalism, the more others, even those mothers whose children were directly impacted by the situation, followed my example. Instead of going up to the podium in a t-shirt and jeans and starting to yell and use profanity, they'd dress professionally and speak articulately and passionately about the issue. As they did this, they were taken seriously and were better positioned to take full advantage of the opportunity to change the system for the better.

We can impact people negatively or positively, but we have to be intentional about it. A positive influencer is there to build up and validate the worth of the individuals around them because they are there to serve them. They see others as more worthy than themselves, and they want to see people succeed. A negative influencer will tear down others so they can elevate themselves.

The other lesson I have learned is that everybody is going to be influenced by you, regardless of whether or not you are trying to affect them. It is your presence that influences others, and it can manifest itself in varying ways. A negatively *persuasive* influencer tries to get you to do something that you really don't want to do. They'll do whatever it takes to get you to move in a direction they want, and it is selfishly motivated. A negatively *dominating* influencer declares, "I don't care. You *are* going to do it." They take over and devalue and intimidate people. But a dominating influencer who is *positive* already has a background and a history of credibility that is reputable, honors others, and is respectful and is usually someone who walks into a space with a certain anointing.

As an influencer in certain arenas, I have shifted the whole conversation without even realizing it. In support of efforts by the Black Mothers Forum to change policies regarding disproportionate disciplinary practices in our schools, I was invited in early 2019 to a legislative session to discuss a bill with one of our state house representatives. It was my first time in such a meeting, and I wanted to take time to observe the room. However, the discussion the lawmakers were having with themselves got to a point where I felt I had to speak up and, in turn, I influenced the conversation. I was nervous and trembling, but I again said what I needed to say with passion and respect. When I was done, I concluded by saying, "I apologize for interrupting your conversation."

Everybody just looked at me in the back of the room. I was met with a glazed stare until one of the policymakers said, "Ms. Wood, we are so sorry. We did not mean—oh my gosh, if this is what you thought? You know what, she is right. We really need to be looking at what is best for the children."

It changed the entire conversation. I listened to them shift the whole dialogue, which was impactful and powerful. My influence in that space was both positive and dominating.

Besides Jesus, the person who has most impacted me as an influencer is Mother Teresa. I have studied how she moved in and out of systems that were averse to women in leadership, especially in the Catholic faith. Her desire to serve God surpassed her fear. She was willing to follow the Lord, take care of the poor and needy in India, and give people dignity. One of the things I like to do is validate people—to *see* them. Mother Teresa saw the man lying on the ground dying of thirst. Everybody was walking around him, and no one noticed but God. He sent her there to kneel down and see the broken man. That validated him. Mother Teresa worked tirelessly with God-given purpose to fulfill her life mission to help those who were dying. Give them a cool glass of water. Pat them on the head with a wet cloth. Give them a cot to lay on. She was dealing with Hinduism, yet she said, "I'm not here to try to convert you. I am here to be the best Christian I can possibly be. You do you, and I'll do me." Her famous saying was, "I am but a pencil in the hand of God." That is how I feel. I feel He can use me as a pencil to write how He wants to influence the story of people's lives.

One of the most influential women in my life is my mother. As a single mom, she always made time to go and advocate for our needs in school. She made sure her two daughters had everything they needed academically to be successful. I loved music, and there was a time I wanted to be a singer. In my seventh-grade choir, I believed I could out sing all the girls and that I should get solos. Yet my choir teacher, a black woman, always gave solo opportunities to other girls who, in my eyes, had weaker voices. My grade in choir was a C, and I could sing. When my mother asked my choir teacher why I had a C in her class, she responded that I had a bad attitude because I thought I was the best singer in her class, so she never gave me solo opportunities.

"Let me get this straight," my mom told her. "My daughter is confident in her voice, and you are penalizing her because she is confident? I have taught my children to be confident because enough people will come against them in the world and try to tear them down. I have done all I can to build them up, so they know who they are. For you to say this is of great concern to me, and we are going to have a big problem. As a matter of fact, I am going to report you to the principal because this is unacceptable."

I never got my solo, but my grade went up—and that was the first time I saw a black mother fighting for her child. It made an impression that informs what I'm doing today.

Finally, I don't recall her name, but I was in eighth grade when a black female audiologist came to my school to speak—and I'll never forget what she said. "As a female, and a black female, in America, life is going to throw everything it can at you to put barriers in your way, so you won't be successful. You have to dig deep and know who you are. I got out of high school and did well, and I went to college. I met a young man there, and we got married at an early age. He was abusive to me. I ended up having three children with this guy while I was still in college, and I knew I wanted to be an audiologist. It was excruciatingly painful to get divorced with three children as a single mother and continue on, but I did it because I knew who I was. My family made sure I knew that."

She concluded, "I'm telling you today who you are. You are bright. You are gifted. You are amazing, and you are stronger than you think you are. If you keep that in mind, you will be successful."

One of the biggest rewards of being an influencer is watching people grow. One of my mothers from the Black Mothers Forum, Simone, is so unique. She is starting to flourish as a motivational speaker in the financial literacy arena, and she has secured a really good job as a result of being coached to go for it. She is becoming the leader that I always knew she was. Simone said I was the only one that could get her to move because she watched me do it first, and she has seen how things open up for me simply because I decided to show up and have continued to move as I am led. That's wonderful to know—because I strive to move in the power and anointing of God's Holy Spirit. I will continue to move as I am led, always mindful that as I move, others are being built up along the way.

My whole mission is to build over a million "buildings" before I die, and those buildings are the people that I come into contact with on a daily basis. I want to build them up in such a way that they are able to live out valued and purposeful lives.

I believe you'll position yourself to be a person of influence through total surrender to the process. It is a journey, and there must be a willingness to be humiliated at times, and to accept that humility, as a way of shaping you into a person of great character. You should not be focused on yourself, but on uplifting the individuals you have been surrounded by or sent to. It is the edification of those individuals that brings forth influence.

The adage rings true. "I don't care how much you know. I care how much you care." If someone sees that you genuinely, authentically care about their well-being, their welfare, and their success, that is when you will have the greatest influence.

Janelle Wood is the founder of the Black Mothers Forum, Inc., a non-profit organization founded in 2016. Janelle also served as a partnership specialist with the U.S. Census Bureau for the 2020 Decennial Census. She holds a bachelor's degree in economics and a master's degree in biblical leadership. Contact Janelle at info@blackmothersforums.com

Made in USA - Kendallville, IN
1209038_9781951501174
12.09.2020 0836